JOLTED SOBER

Also by Sylvia Cary
It Must Be Five O'Clock Somewhere

JOLTED SOBER

GETTING TO THE
Moment of Clarity
IN THE RECOVERY
FROM ADDICTION

Sylvia Cary, MA, MFCC

Lowell House
• LOS ANGELES •
Contemporary Books
• CHICAGO •

For Jessica, Claudia and Lance
with Love
And for Bill W. and Dr. Bob S.
and Their Two Million "Wounded Healers"
with Gratitude

Library of Congress Cataloging-in-Publication Data

Cary, Sylvia.
    Jolted sober : getting to the moment of clarity in the recovery
from addiction
        p. cm.
    ISBN 0-929923-06-5
    ISBN 0-929923-23-5 ppbk.
    1. Alcoholics—Rehabilitation. 2. Mind and body.
    3. Life change events. 4. Self-actualization
(Psychology) I. Title.
HV5278.C37 1989   89-12532
616.86 ' 10651—dc20   CIP

Copyright © 1989 by RGA Publishing Group, Inc.

Lowell House
1875 Century Park East
Los Angeles, CA 90067

Design: Robert S. Tinnon
Manufactured in the United States of America
10   9   8   7   6   5   4   3   2

Contents

The Day I
Was Jolted Sober

> In medicine, as in life, until the mind has been pre-
> pared to see something, it will pass unnoticed, as in-
> visible as though it did not exist.
>
> —*Ovid, ancient Roman poet*

There's no such thing as an instant cure. At least that's what
they told me in graduate school when I was studying clinical
psychology. Recovery happens in a slow, step-by-step, linear
way over time, they said. People get better in bits.

My first job out of school was as a rookie staff psychologist
at Boston State Hospital, a huge mental institution that at the
time housed 3,000 patients. While there I'd occasionally hear
stories about patients who claimed to have been instantly cured
of psychosis or depression. Either they or their doctors referred
to them as "conversion experiences," and that's where they lost
me. Coming from an agnostic family, I was uncomfortable with
a religious-sounding word such as *conversion*. So whenever
these stories popped up I dismissed them as quackish, too un-
sophisticated for my tastes. I put them out of my mind.

Over the next few years there were some major changes in
my personal life. I fell in love with a psychiatrist I'd met on a
blind date, and we got married. We had two little girls. We
moved to California. And, after many years of writing things
that didn't sell, I sold some articles and got a book contract. I
could now call myself a Real Writer.

But somewhere in there I ran into a slight snag: a drinking problem. At least I called it a drinking problem until I learned that's just a nice way of saying *alcoholism*. It started off simply enough with a martini before dinner, then progressed to martinis before dinner, then to martinis *instead* of dinner.

Each morning I said never again. But each evening at five o'clock, like Pavlov's dog, I arrived home from work and, salivating at the sound of my own keys in the lock, threw down my purse and headed straight for the gin.

My husband, like so many physicians (even today, unfortunately) knew next to nothing about addiction. He'd had a total of three hours on the subject in medical school. Like me, he'd been taught that alcoholism is a symptom of an underlying emotional disorder that could be fixed with in-depth psychotherapy. When it came to my own drinking, since I was already seeing a psychotherapist and talking about my problems, I figured I was taking care of it. Or so I thought. The only problem was I never mentioned to my therapist that I drank.

It took only eight years for gin to wreck my marriage, derail my writing career (I never wrote that first book), interfere with my ability to parent my two daughters, and begin to erode my health.

I still didn't get the drift. I decided it was my husband's fault that I drank, so I left him. Hiding behind the women's-liberation lingo of the early 1970s, I told people I had to go out and "find myself."

What I found was more gin.

Over the next two years it got to be ridiculous. I couldn't go one day without drinking. And in the end, having long ago lost faith in psychiatry as the answer, I decided to attend a local self-help group meeting for alcoholics to see what it was all about. I didn't expect much and planned to give it only one shot.

Arriving a few minutes late, I sat down in the back. I felt silly being there and knew I was probably wasting my time. How could something as superficial as a meeting help me with a drinking problem that was so obviously complex? Even if I stayed, since of course there are no instant cures, I knew it would take two to five years to make a dent in my situation. What made it worse was the fact that I could still feel the urge to drink lurking inside of me, like an organ in my body. Later I was to learn that another name for that "urge" is *obsession*— and the obsession *is* the alcoholism. All I was aware of at the time was that as long as the obsession was there—and I couldn't imagine it *not* being there— I was doomed.

Then, suddenly, "it" happened.

It was right after the coffee break. I was listening to the speaker, a TV actor. He was funny, and I was laughing, something I hadn't done in a long time. The next thing I was aware of was a little thought that seemed to arise spontaneously from somewhere in the right side of my brain and waft its way gently across my mind. The thought was, "They're sober; I'm not. I think I'll listen and do what they say." By the time the thought arrived at the left side of my brain my whole world had changed.

That was more than sixteen years ago. I haven't had a drink since.

What hapened? Well, what happened was that I had an instant "cure"—exactly the kind of thing I'd always been told didn't exist.

That idle thought had triggered a kind of click inside, which resulted in nothing less than a world-view shift. I saw the same old stuff of my life differently. In the addiction field it's called a *moment of clarity*, but at the time I didn't know such an event existed. In a flash I'd seen clearly that I was an alcoholic and that the solution was really simple beyond words: Stop drinking alcohol!

It struck me as a dazzling revelation. So long as I didn't drink alcohol I'd have no drinking problem. Period. No need to dig into my childhood. No need to dredge up the "reasons" I drank before I could stop it. Even more important was the fact that when I looked inside myself for that familiar old gin urge, the obsession, it was gone. It had simply disappeared.

It was a powerful moment in my life, to date, *the* moment. It came out of nowhere and turned my life right-side *up*. (It had been upside down during the eight years I drank.) I knew it was "important," but I didn't know anything more about it. I decided to find out. I began looking in the indexes of books to find something that would explain how an eight-year gin addiction could disappear in a split second without a trace. The books in which I looked (mostly contemporary psychology and self-help) didn't help much. Few had anything to say about sudden change. In fact, it soon became clear that Western psychology, despite a great concern with health and healing, scarcely acknowledged that this event, which had just changed my life, even existed. When sudden change happened, it was considered a fluke and something to be suspicious of or to be filed under "religious" and forgotten. Outside of some of the self-help groups, it looked as if it was one of the best-kept secrets in the alcoholism-treatment field.

Although I was hearing about similar experiences from other recovering addicts and alcoholics, I was becoming increasingly frustrated by the lack of "agreement" on this issue in the literature. As yet I'd had no exposure to Eastern philosophy, but that changed when a man named Bruno took me to hear the Indian philosopher Krishnamurti at the Santa Monica Civic Auditorium, where they used to have the Academy Awards. Although I didn't understand a word Krishnamurti said, I bought one of his books and opened it. In the middle of it I read: "There is no such thing as a cure, there is only a shift in world view." "That's it!" I said to myself. "That's what I experienced when I got jolted sober." Finally I'd found somebody who "agreed" with me. My experience *was* real.

That gave me the push to continue my research and poking around, which has culminated in this book.

The search began in my own recovery meetings (which I still attend), and it soon became obvious that I wasn't the only person to have this kind of quick addiction cure. (The addiction field doesn't like to use the word *cure*, so when I use it visualize it in italics.)

I visited self-help groups for eating disorders, for smoking and for gambling, and I heard about jolt cures in each of these places. I also heard about them from my private patients (I knew how to spot them now) and from the patients in the chemical-dependency treatment center in which I worked as a psychotherapist. Quick-cure stories began to jump out at me from TV talk shows, movies, books, and newspapers. I heard people talking about them at parties. I eavesdropped in restaurants and heard about them there. It didn't seem to matter what the addiction was (you could fill in the blank with the name), the healing process was always the same: Some stimuli or event (internal or external) triggered a moment of clarity within an addicted person, and the result was a lasting recovery.

This is the book I wish I'd had to read sixteen years ago. This is the book I was looking for that might have helped explain what happened to me. It's also the book I would have consulted when I wanted to tackle some of my other addictions and when I started working as a therapist with other addicts and drunks.

In researching *Jolted Sober* I had to push through a lot of my own linear thinking. I'm still doing it. Sometimes it feels like pushing a boulder uphill.

The material on these pages has been collected in bits and pieces. A sentence from a book would jump out at me here, a quote from a newspaper article there. I even carried 3-by-5-inch file cards with me to the movies in case I heard a snatch of dialogue that was jolt-sober related. I'm sure long after this book is published I'll run across some of those file cards in coat pockets.

While most people use the term *moment of clarity* to describe the experience, other terms are used as well, such as *moment of truth*, *turning point*, or *surrender*.

It appears that there are actually two phases of addiction recovery: the pre-jolt phase (which can include abstinence) and the post-jolt phase. Those who have had a moment of clarity or jolt cure end up with a more comfortable and longer-lasting sobriety than those who are still "biting the bullet." If pre-jolt people don't eventually have a moment of clarity, chances are they won't get sober or, even if they do, they'll "slip," meaning they'll drink or use again.

Relapse is a terrible problem, far worse than people realize. But, like the emperor's new clothes, nobody talks about that part of it. Yet most alcoholics and addicts relapse. Some say four out of five fall by the wayside. Others say it's more like nine out of ten. From my own experience, I'd say it's nine out of ten. Somebody once compared Alcoholics Anonymous, the largest of all the self-help groups, to a giant tube. To have reached its current worldwide membership of 2 million people means that 20 million people had to have marched into one end of the tube and eighteen million out the other.

So obviously just *getting* clean and sober isn't enough. The trick is in staying clean and sober. And what that takes is a jolt cure.

Just what *is* a jolt recovery? What causes it? Why has it been one of healing's best-kept open secrets for thousands of years? Can you recover without a moment of clarity? Can you have more than one? And most important of all: If a jolt healing is so important for lasting addiction healing, can you *make* a moment of clarity happen in yourself or in somebody else?

That's what this book is all about.

PART 1

JOLTED SOBER

CHAPTER 1

What Does "Jolted Sober" Mean?

> I was 29. I'd been in prison since I was 19. One evening I looked out into the yard and saw a beautiful sunset over one of the towers. Suddenly, I understood my whole life. I felt all the guilt, all the remorse, and saw my responsibility in the matter, all in one second. It sobered me up and changed me forever.
> —*Niles, 39, sober 10 years*

ANYTIME, ANYWHERE

It could happen at any time. It could happen to an alcoholic at an Alcoholics Anonymous meeting. It could happen to a cocaine addict at a treatment center. It could happen to a crack user while sitting on a curb. It could happen to a pill abuser while having coffee with a friend. Or while jogging. Or admiring a sunset. Or being beaten up. Or watching TV. Or having a car wreck.

You hear something, think something, feel something, read something, remember something, notice something, or even say something—and that's it. Suddenly there's a kind of click inside, an aha! For a split moment you see clearly, as though for the first time. And what you see enables you to stop drinking, drugging, overeating, smoking, spending, gambling—sometimes forever.

It's as though you'd been jolted sober.

No matter how far down you've gone; no matter what your personal history; no matter what drug you're addicted to or how many times in the past you've tried and failed to sober up, suddenly one day "it" happens, and the obsession (which *is* the addiction) drops away. Once that occurs, you're on the mend. To those outside the addiction-recovery field this sounds crazy, snake-oil stuff. An instant cure for chemical dependency? That's definitely a hard sell.

We think we "know" there's no quick fix for such a deep-rooted and complex problem. We hear statements to this effect all the time: "There are no overnight cures"; "Recovery takes time"; "You can't expect magic, you know." And when we have an example of an instant recovery right in front of us, we rush to explain it away: "Well, *sure* he's not drinking anymore, but that was just willpower."

THERE'S EVIDENCE

On a TV talk show to publicize his book, *Love, Medicine and Miracles,* physician/author Bernie S. Siegel, M.D., said there are some 3,500 articles in the medical literature about people who have gotten over incurable physical diseases "instantly" via an "existential inner shift." Almost every physician has known such a case. The idea of spontaneous remissions from physical illnesses has attained a certain level of acceptance, but we're still not accustomed to hearing about instant cures from addictions. Yet there are thousands, maybe hundreds of thousands, of examples of such jolt healings available to us. They're not called that, of course. They're called tamer things like *moment of clarity* or *surrender* experiences, but they mean the same thing.

> I call it a moment of transformation. I went from one kind of life to another kind of life in one moment, all as the result of a doctor standing at the end of my bed [in an alcohol-treatment center] and saying some words to me.
> —*actor Patrick O'Neal in an educational film about Antabuse*

I became very emotional. I got to my feet. "I'm Betty, and I'm an alcoholic!" I heard myself saying, and I couldn't believe it. I was trembling; another defense had cracked.

—*Betty Ford in* The Times of My Life

I realized with startling clarity for the first time the simplest of ideas—so simple but so all-important: I didn't drink because I had problems; I had problems because I drank!

—*Barnaby Conrad in "My Four Weeks at the Betty Ford Center,"*
Los Angeles Times Magazine

I went from black and white to color in a split second.

—*Barry, 40s, sober six years*

Rx: A MOMENT OF CLARITY

Swiss psychoanalyst Carl Jung was well aware of the importance of a jolt-healing experience to insure lasting sobriety. The story goes that a wealthy American alcoholic named Rowland H. (his last name isn't known) went to Switzerland to go into analysis with Jung to cure his alcoholism, but to no avail. After a year, Jung told Rowland that he couldn't help him, that his only salvation was a vital spiritual experience.

That's a hard prescription to fill! But that's exactly what happened. Rowland returned to America, joined a philosophical, evangelical organization called the Oxford Groups founded on "right living," had his spiritual experience, and did indeed stop drinking. Rowland told his friend Ebby Thatcher all about it, and Ebby joined and also stopped drinking. Then Ebby told his friend Bill Wilson, and later Bill Wilson had *his* famous spiritual awakening in his room at the Charles B. Towns Hospital in New York, stopped drinking, and went on to start Alcoholics Anonymous. The rest is AA history. Today the organization is worldwide and has two million members.

For the past fifteen years I've been collecting examples of jolt recoveries from addictions. I get them from my work as a psychotherapist in a chemical-dependency treatment center, from private patients, from people in audiences wherever I speak, from peers in my own alcoholism-recovery group meetings, from books, magazines, newspapers, movies, friends, parties, and from eavesdropping.

To give you the flavor of the jolted-sober experience, here are some typical examples from my files:

> I had a moment of clarity. I realized I didn't have to stay sober the rest of my life. I only had to stay sober one day at a time
> *—Mike, 77, sober 41 years*

> Walking to the corner mailbox one day it hit me like a flash that every letter I mailed was costing me about five dollars—the price of the stamp plus the price of the vodka I needed to drink just to get up the courage to leave the house. That's the moment I *knew* I was an alcoholic. I turned myself in to Alcoholics Anonymous that night and haven't had a drink since.
> *—Elizabeth, 44, sober 17 years*

> It was Super Bowl Sunday. I was at dinner. I took two bites and threw up—and that was it. Half an hour later I was on the phone to AA. After the first moment of surrender I had second thoughts, but I had committed myself. It was an ironclad commitment.
> *—Dirk, 40s, sober 19 years*

> At 29 I was using a lot of cocaine, even in front of my four-year-old daughter. One day she blurted out, "You're going to die when you're 30, Mommy!" At that moment, the obsession for cocaine went away.
> *—Ella, 30, sober 10 months*

THE QUICK-FIX TABOO

Until the last decade or so, there's been a kind of taboo on the subject of instant healings, at least in this culture. The notion that something can happen for no apparent reason mystifies us and makes us uncomfortable.

The taboo has kept us from seeing a truth that's been hiding right under our noses all along: Jolt cures really do happen.

In his book "The Transformation" George Leonard says, "One of the more powerful taboo mechanisms is simply not providing a vocabulary for the experience to be tabooed." Sociologist/writer/priest Andrew Greeley calls this taboo a "scientific iron curtain" that has made many people who have actually *had* quick cures keep quiet about them. At the Alister Hardy Research Center, Oxford, England (formerly the Religious Experience Research Unit at Manchester College), where to date they've examined close to 6,000 religious, transformational, peak, and healing experiences, some of their interviewees complained that when they approached members of the clergy to discuss their experiences, they were advised to seek psychiatric help.

> To pretend that [such events] do not occur to ordinary people in everyday life is like a Victorian novelist pretending that sexual intercourse does not occur. Either sham is, to say the least, nonscientific—if not inhuman.
>
> —*Rev. Andrew Greeley*

THERE'S A WORD FOR IT

> The difference between the right word and almost the right word is the difference between lightning and lightning bug.
>
> —*Mark Twain*

What do these terms all have in common: *moment of truth, conversion, religious experience, spiritual awakening, mystical experience, illumination, gestalt formation, grace, vision, born-again experience, insight, transformation, getting it, enlightenment, awareness, miracle, felt shift, peak experience, convictional event, cosmic consciousness, quantum leap, divine intervention, a greater reality, left-right brain shift, gift of the guru, revelation, deep knowing, sudden decision, inner feeling, flash point, inner voice,* and, of course, *moment of clarity, turning point,* and *surrender?*

These are *all* terms people use when trying to describe the experience of being suddenly changed or jolted sober. But none really do the trick. Our language here is woefully inadequate. Instant healing has never been an easy subject to talk about. Each person, group, sect, field, or discipline latches onto one or the other of these inadequate words or phrases for the jolted-sober experience and doesn't recognize that some other group, using a different word, is talking about the same thing.

As a result, there has been little group-to-group, field-to-field, or culture-to-culture communication on the subject.

To insure easier dialogue, I wanted to come up with an umbrella term that would make it clear that what I'm talking about is recovery that happens *fast,* often when one least expects it. My first choice was the *flash experience,* but too many people associated that with "flashers" in raincoats, or with LSD flashbacks, so I returned to the drawing board. *Jolted sober* was the result. It will have to do until we develop a better vocabulary for the instant-healing phenomenon.

GOOD NEWS FOR SKEPTICS

> It almost doesn't matter what's done, astonishing cures. . .can still result—plus *faith* isn't even a requirement.
> —*F. W. Knowles, M. D.*

For those of you who have heard that it's the power of positive thinking, or faith, or a fighting spirit, that brings on miraculous healings, here's some good news. It's not. None of these things is a prerequisite for a jolt cure—nor is it even enough. Even if you're a skeptic and haven't a shred of belief that what you're doing will "work," still you're as likely to have a jolt recovery as the next person. It's not that there's anything wrong with positive thinking; it's just that it's not necessary. You can even be a relapser, or be considered a hopeless case, and still be jolted sober.

I was in 57 different alcoholism-treatment centers and recovery homes. In 12 years the longest period of sobriety I could put together was 41 days. They'd all given up on me. *I'd* given up on me. Then one day I just said to myself, "I think I'll work the program," and that was it.

—Joanie, 35, sober 18 months

It appears that it's not faith and belief that causes healing, it's healing that causes faith and belief. We've had it backwards all along.

ROMANCING A JOLT RECOVERY

You can lead an alcoholic to treatment, but you can't make him (or her) stop drinking. However, you *can* increase the odds. Learning how to do that is the purpose of this book.

I call it "romancing" the jolt-recovery experience. I purposely use the word *romance* to make it clear that in matters of healing, just as in matters of the heart, there are never any guarantees. But there are ways to "court" recovery.

While there are endless methods of romancing jolt cures, I've taken what I consider to be the most effective romancing approaches and organized them into seven basic categories, which I've sketched out below. In Part 2, there is an entire chapter on each of the methods.

One: The first approach, and the one I think is the most important, is **People Ways**. This means putting your body where they're talking about your primary problem—your addiction. Take yourself to a recovery group meeting, a lecture, a class—anyplace where there are *other people* meeting to discuss that addiction—and stay there until the meeting is over.

People have been getting well in communities and groups since cave days, so there must be something to it. Today's self-help-group explosion recognizes the value of people contact in healing. In fact, the very foundation of Alcoholics Anonymous is "one drunk talking to another." It even works for people who say they don't like groups.

Two: The next method is **Physical Ways**. The mathematician

Jacques Hadamard once said that the legs are "the wheels of thought," by which he meant that sometimes being in action physically is the best way to trigger creativity. It's also a good way to trigger a jolt cure. This chapter is for those who are physical types and are more likely to heal "on the run."

Three: **Intellectual Ways** is for the scholars and information junkies among you, those heady types who don't feel that anything is real until you see it written down. You always hear that information never changed anybody. Not true. I have many examples in which people got sober right after reading an article, hearing a pertinent statistic, or picking up a piece of information. So read all about your addiction, and maybe you'll think your way into a sudden healing.

Four: In **Quiet Ways**, we'll discuss ways the addicted person can get past his or her busy mind and tap into the inner, intuitive wisdom. We'll focus on certain techniques, such as meditation, contemplation, prayer, sleep, and even dreams, that are often successful at shaking loose some inner truth that triggers a jolt cure.

Five: **Brain Ways** talks about nondrug ways of altering brain chemistry, which may trigger a moment-of-clarity healing. Aside from the techniques already discussed, any one of which can affect the chemistry of the brain, such things as acupuncture, biofeedback, food, and vitamins have all been known to alter brain chemistry and consciousness and stimulate recoveries.

Six: **Contrary Ways** talks about taking actions that by their very unrelatedness or oppositeness to standard treatments can actually trigger jolt healings—going on an adventure instead of going to a chemical-dependency unit for the fifth time, or the popular AA paradox "The cure for alcoholism is drinking."

Finally, Seven: **Hitting Bottom**. This is the chapter of last resort. It's the chapter that slippers and relapsers should probably look at first for encouragement because it will show them that there are no hopeless cases, only cases who haven't been lucky enough yet to stumble across the right trigger for *their* jolt cure. But it's out there. It may take one more drink or one more crisis or one more humiliation to get there, but if that's what it takes, that's what it takes.

Keep in mind that our goal here is *not* personal transformation, spirituality, or even happiness. Our goal here is instant healing—period. If any of the foregoing happens as a side effect, terrific, but that's not our focus. If you're using a romancing technique, and it hasn't led you to a jolt cure within a reasonable (we'll discuss what "reasonable" means later) amount of time, drop it and try something else. Or keep it, but make another technique number one.

In Part 3 we look at life *after* the jolted-sober experience. In "Maintaining Your Jolt Recovery," you'll see that just because you've had a jolt healing doesn't mean you're home free. People often relapse, which is why Alcoholics Anonymous and other recovery groups don't like to use the word *cure*, why they say recover*ing* instead of recover*ed* alcoholic or addict. It reminds them that their hold on sobriety is tenuous at best.

So even though the jolt recovery happens instantly, maintaining it takes a lifetime.

The chapter about "Helping Others" is of interest because most of us, addicted or not, know somebody who *is* whom we'd like to help.

Some of you are family members or "concerned others." Some are professional healers. And some are "wounded healers," as I am, treating alcoholics as well as being recovering alcoholics yourselves.

How can we go about helping somebody *else* get jolted sober? That's what "Helping Others" looks into.

THERE'S RESISTANCE

If heaven is always available to us, what stops us?
—*Abraham Maslow, psychologist*

You have the rest of your life to become the person you were meant to be—or defend who you are.
—*said at AA meeting by Clint, 51, sober 22 years*

I was jolted sober accidentally. That's lucky because I never would have gone looking for it. First, because I didn't know the experience existed. Second, because I'd have resisted it. Most people, even those who want to change, have some built-in resistance to it. It goes with the territory. We resist, even though it's change for the better. Usually we'll keep right on resisting until life knocks the wind out of our sails. That's because it's painful and irksome to change. It feels like too much trouble. Our heads say, "Watch out! Something awful and terrible is about to happen!" And the closer we get to our moment of clarity, the more uncomfortable we get. Many of us simply bolt. Some of us try again later. Some of us don't. Some resistance is so cowardly it lasts forever.

Here's a case where the resistance continued even *after* the jolt cure:

> I don't like this, but I guess I'm home. I guess maybe I don't have to drink anymore.
>
> —*Lucy, 36, sober 4 years*

In my own case, much as I feared the pain of *not* drinking, I was even more afraid of the pain of continuing. I was afraid of what would happen to me if I kept on downing all those little glasses full of gin.

> If at any moment you find yourself hesitating . . . putting off until tomorrow trying some new piece of behavior that you *could* do today . . . then all you need to do is glance over your left shoulder, and there will be a fleeting shadow. That shadow represents your death, and at any moment it might step forward, place its hand on your shoulder and take you. So that the act that you are presently engaged in might be your very last act and therefore fully representative of you as your last act on this planet. . . It is indulgent to hesitate and act as though you are immortal. . .
>
> —*Carlos Castaneda*

So with this in mind, let's move on.

CHAPTER 2

The Nature of the Beast

> It can be compared with nothing so well as a dazzling flash of lightning in a dark night, bringing the landscape which had been hidden into clear view.
> —*Richard M. Bucke, M.D., in* Cosmic Consciousness

In order to romance a jolt recovery from addiction, we need to know more about it. What, for example, does it feel like to be jolted sober?

Some use analogies, saying a moment of clarity is "like a drop of catalytic fluid in a highly saturated chemical solution," "like a full teacup just at the moment it runs over," "like the sudden shift of a kaleidoscope pattern," "like a pinhole into paradise," or this:

> It was like a creative act. One minute my life was a jumble and in the next minute I was totally changed.
> —*musician Lionel Richie*

And Bucke again:

> It's as if a veil were, with one sharp jerk, torn from the eyes of the mind, letting sight pierce through.

Some say it doesn't feel so much like an *event* as a *thought*— a thought with a little jolt to it. Others describe it as a deep, inner knowing, a "gut feeling." And still others experience it as physical, as a brain shift or click, something similar to what

11

you might feel looking at these classic psychology textbook pictures below.

Figure 1

Did you see a pretty young woman or an old hag? Now what about Figure 2?

Figure 2

Was it two profiles? or a vase? Did you notice a feeling in your brain as the picture you *didn't* see suddenly revealed itself? Now practice shifting back and forth. Can you feel something happen in your head as you first see one picture, then the other? (You can't see both at once.)

Well, on a much larger scale the same thing happens when we have a jolt cure. Suddenly we perceive something in life that we'd been blind to before.

IT'S HAPPENING ALL OVER

We usually think of instant healings as rare. They are not. Instant cures happen all over the world—and always have. Today it's not unusual to find people who have had more than one. Whole families can have moment-of-clarity experiences. I have one case on file in which the mother, the father, and the daughter all had jolt healings.

Clearly we are more open to the quick-cure phenomenon today than we have been in the past (except in some highly religious settings). This gives us a wonderful opportunity to learn more about it.

THE CAUSE VERSUS CAUSELESS DEBATE

> Behold, I tell you a mystery. We shall not all sleep, but we shall all be changed, in a moment, in the twinkling of an eye.
> —*St. Paul the Apostle*

Jolt healings appear abrupt because, from our point of view at least, they are discontinuous or "causeless." There is no apparent step-by-step reason for them.

A lot of us are bothered by this. We can't accept it because we're still a linear culture, and we like to dissect things. For every effect (like instant addiction recovery) we say there *must* be a cause—that people just can't get well for no reason.

The opposite side says, "Of course there are such things as causeless events." A coincidence is a causeless event. So is synchronicity. So why not instant healing?

Actually both sides are right. During the pre-jolt phase the jolt-healing process does indeed appear to be step by step and linear up to a point, but then something—it can be anything—triggers a shift, too fast to even measure, and healing is the result. Then the last phase, the post-jolt phase, becomes linear and step by step again. It looks like this:

| pre-jolt phase | jolt | post-jolt phase |

History tells us that the Buddha got his enlightenment or jolt transformation instantly, in a flash, but only after he'd studied for 14 years. Afterward, he maintained the experience by teaching and spiritual practices. Martin Luther's "lightning bolt" experience also came after much work and was maintained by more work still. Twentieth-century philosopher and spiritual master Swami Baba Muktananda got his awakening in a split second, but it was after 25 years of devotion and study.

HIGH DRAMA VERSUS THE SUBTLE SIGN

When most people think of a "conversion experience" (another name for jolt change), they think of something dramatic, like the conversion of St. Paul on the road to Damascus. Paul, after years of being an obsessed persecutor of the early Christians, had a dramatic and sudden change of heart, via the same phenomenon that removes the obsession to pursue an addiction:

> As he journeyed it came to pass that he drew nigh unto Damascus. Suddenly there shone round about him a light out of heaven, and he fell upon the earth and heard a voice saying unto him, "Saul, Saul, why persecutest thou me?"
>
> —*From "Paul," in Bucke's* Cosmic Consciousness

Others in history have had similar high-drama change experiences. One was AA's co-founder, Bill Wilson:

> Suddenly, the room lit up with a great white light. I was caught up into an ecstasy which there are no words to describe . . . And then it burst upon me that I was a free man.
> —*Bill Wilson, quoted in* AA Comes of Age

Here are some contemporary dramas:

> I aimed the gun at my husband, but changed my mind. Instead, I put it to my head and pulled the trigger, but it didn't go off. I pulled the trigger again, and again it didn't go off. "What's wrong with this thing?" I said. I pointed the gun at the wall, and I blew a hole right through it. At that moment in a flash I realized I was supposed to live.
> —*Pat, 40s, sober six years*

> I was on my motorcycle, drunk on booze, stoned on grass, and paranoid as all get-out. A pickup truck hit me, and there I was sailing through the air, with no helmet. When I landed I rolled past a gas station, a McDonald's, and a taco stand before I came to a complete stop. I haven't had a drink since that day.
> —*Dick, 30s, sober eight years*

Unfortunately, stories such as these can be inhibiting for the rest of us. We think that a healing or change is only "real" if it's dramatic. Apparently many early AAs felt that their own healings weren't valid. To reassure them, an appendix was added to later editions of the AA "bible," *Alcoholics Anonymous:*

> The terms "spiritual experience" and "spiritual awakening" are used many times in this book . . . Our first printing gave many readers the impression that [changes] must be in the nature of sudden and spectacular upheavals. Happily for everyone, this conclusion is erroneous . . . Such transformations, though frequent, are by no means the rule.

Judging from my own personal collection of a few hundred jolted-sober experiences, most are *not* dramatic. Many, in fact, are so subtle they managed to nearly escape the attention of the people having them:

> It wasn't a kaboom or a voice in thunder. It was just a feeling that came over me, and I said to myself, "Maybe, after all this, there's a way for me now." And that phrase turned my whole life around.
>
> —*John, 60s, sober 21 years*

> After downing two vodkas just because the phone rang, it occurred to me that social drinkers didn't do things like that—and I called AA.
>
> *Karen, 40s, sober two months*

FINDING THE RIGHT TRIGGER

> Something has to *click* in your head. You have to *get* it.
>
> —*Oprah on* The Oprah Winfrey Show, *November 1988, talking about her 67-pound weight loss*

> There is something that gives a click inside of us, a bell that strikes twelve . . . .
>
> *William James, psychologist, in* The Will To Believe

Jolt recoveries, different as they are from one another, all have one thing in common—they're triggered by something. In each case, some last straw, usually accidental, turns out to be the doorway to healing. The trick, of course, is in finding the right last straw.

A trigger can be anything—a dream, a memory, a feeling, a trauma, a near-death experience, a smell, a look on a child's face, a snatch of movie dialogue, the words of a song, a piece of information, a confrontation, fright, hunger, fatigue, deep breathing, music, mountains, a painting, chanting, a Zen koan, dancing, yoga, running, even somebody else's throwaway line. There are as many triggers as snowflakes, no two alike.

The Slot Machine Analogy

I like to think of addicted people as silver-dollar slot machines, each one uniquely set up for a different number of silver dollars before there's a "jackpot" or jolt cure. Some people may need only one silver dollar to hit a jackpot, some a hundred, some a thousand. (If your addiction is gambling, I apologize for this analogy and suggest you use the "last straw" idea instead. Except for the payoff, it's basically the same thing.)

Some Trigger Tales

In telling about their jolt cures, most people only hint at the possible triggers, so it's hard to tell what they were. In the examples below I've italicized the *probable* triggers or last straws—those that occurred *just* before the healing process kicked in.

I went to a psychiatrist. *When she asked* how she could help me, I said: "I have a lot of problems, but until we address the problem of my drug and alcohol use, I don't know which problems are really real!" She was shocked I'd said that right out like that, and so was I. I don't know where the words came from. My whole life changed in that flash awareness. I checked myself into a treatment center, and I've been clean and sober ever since.

Lynn, 40s, sober seven years

At my first AA meeting a man said, "Are you allergic to anything?" I said yes, many things, and *when he said*, "Well, do you think you could be allergic to alcohol?" the clarity hit me and was a great relief. At that moment I knew I was an alcoholic and I went for help.

—Anna, 50s, sober eight months

I wasn't at the AA meeting for myself. I was there as a translator for a German AA member who was the invited speaker. I was saying, "*He* couldn't stop drinking; *he* was angry; *he* did such and such." So went the translation from me. Then, *when the speaker* began describing how he continued to think alcoholically, I found myself changing to *I*: *I* was thinking alcoholically. *I* didn't expect anything good to happen, and so on. After that night I never drank again!

— Bill S., age 45, sober seven years

After being picked up from the floor many times by my doctor, this time I called him and *he said* "Are you ready?" I said yes—and I knew I was.

— Dale, 69, sober 25 years

When I heard Diana Ross singing "It's My Turn" on the radio, that did it. I said to myself, "Yeah, it's my turn."

— Lisa, 31, sober three years

My daughter *asked me* not to drink, and I heard myself say to her, "Well, just tell your friends that Mother is an alcoholic." I couldn't believe I'd said that, but I knew it was true. I went to AA three months later and haven't had to take a drink since.

—Winnie, 40s, sober four years

When she told me I could lose weight if I got sober, she appealed to my vanity and I decided to give it a whirl.

—Bob, 50s, sober 14 years

The I-Just-Decided-to-Quit Clue

In the next example, the trigger isn't obvious. It's hidden in the words "I decided." In fact, whenever you hear a recovering person say they "just decided to quit," or words to that effect, your ears should perk up. It's often a clue that they've had a jolt cure.

The moment *I made up my mind* to go through with the process, I had the curious feeling that my alcoholic condition was relieved, as in fact it proved to be.

—Fred's story in Alcoholics Anonymous

I had a change of attitude. I went from negative to positive, and I knew I was going to be okay.

—Taylor, 20s, sober three years

My moment of clarity came when my two grandchildren were a few months old, and *I just decided* that I would like to stay around awhile and see their growth and development through sober eyes.
—*Stefan, 65, sober 11 years*

It only stands to reason that in the past this man must have had some equally compelling reasons to stop drinking. Why now? The best answer I can give you is *timing*.

In healing, timing is everything.

Another thing to remember about triggers is that they aren't causes and can't be counted on to "work" a second time. They won't. The only reason they worked at the time is because the timing was right.

THE AFTER-JOLT SIGNS

How do you know if you've had a jolt recovery? Is it like being in love? Do you "just know"?

If you're an alcoholic or addict the proof is in the pudding: You no longer drink or use. It's that simple. The second thing is, it's not that hard. Post-jolt people don't find abstinence uncomfortable.

There's no such thing as a jolt recovery that doesn't work. They all, by definition, "work." So if you're still practicing your addiction, it wasn't a jolt cure; it was just a good idea whose time hadn't yet come. Try again.

Most jolt healings have some other typical aftereffects:

A Burden Lifted

One of the most common aftereffects of the jolted-sober experience is the sense of relief, of a burden being lifted:

It was like getting a huge Santa Claus pack off my back.
—*Benny, 19, sober five months*

At my first AA meeting I felt an instant lifting of a burden, and I had a light, floating feeling and a certainty inside that I'd never have to drink again.

—Judy, 48, sober eight years

Suddenly I felt this cocoon of serenity; it lasted for three days, and I didn't even *want* a drink. Now I know that was the obsession being removed.

—Helen, 72, sober 30 years

A load weighing a thousand pounds came oft my back.

—recovering alcoholic woman's story, "Stars Don't Fall," in Alcoholics Anonymous

When I realized it was time to take my drinking seriously and *stop* it, I began to cry. People kept saying, "Are you all right?" I was *fine*. I was crying from relief, like a burden had been lifted. I felt lighter and freer.

—Sheila, 32, sober six years

When I walked into the AA office, I was an atheist. A woman there said to me, "Why not try God?" and I thought, "Sure, why *not*? I've tried everything else." Immediately I felt a huge burden lifted. I felt lighter. When I left and walked down the street, the street was lighter. And I knew I'd found the answer.

—Tony, 50s, sober 15 years

Hope

A jolt healing can leave you with a sense of optimism instead of negativism. There's hope now and a destination:

I'd been like a ship lost at sea, but after I had my moment of truth I suddenly had a direction. I knew where I was going. I knew it would take work to get there, but I was ready and willing to go through whatever discomfort I'd have to go through to reach my destination.

—Edith, sober 17 years

Timelessness

Many describe a sense of transcending or of being "outside time" during even the briefest moment-of-clarity experiences. Past, present, and future suddenly appear as one. They can "see" themselves in the future in a healed state as though they were already there:

> I was standing there, drunk, yelling at my husband, trying to make him understand me, when suddenly this calm came over me. That's when I knew that my drinking was over and I'd never be drunk again. It was as though I could look down the road and see myself sober. All that remained was working out the details—like first I had to throw up.
>
> —*Thelma, 41, sober two years*

Responsibility

Most pre-jolt alcoholics and addicts refuse to accept personal responsibility for actions; most post-jolt people accept it gladly:

> I woke up and knew with such clarity; it was as though it had hit me in the face: Nobody *did* anything bad to me ever. My mother and father loved me. My bosses and friends had gone out of their way to help me. My wife had put up with years of me. Nobody *put* me in jail or *made* me drive too fast or *made* me drive drunk. I knew I was totally responsible for that . . . I walked out into the living room and said to my wife and my brother: "I don't care what anybody says, I'm an alcoholic and I need help."
>
> —*Ned, sober 15 years*

Victim No More

Another telltale sign of the addicted person is playing victim. They're right, everybody else is wrong—others are to blame for their being miserable and drunk. Usually a jolt recovery alters this dramatically.

> I read a book about reincarnation called *Many Mansions* by Gina Cerminara. When I closed the book, I said to myself, "Now it begins," and I realized that there was justice, there was mercy, there was balance in the universe. I stopped being a *victim* to anything. Since then, I've been sober and my life has been ruled by one of these flashes after another.
>
> —*Debbie, 40s, sober 14 years*

Service

Many of the great philosophies and religions of the world stress "service" to others as a part of the healing process. The addiction-recovery field does this, too. And people who've had jolt healings seem to feel an impulse to reach out and teach others, just as St. Paul did. In AA and the other "twelve-step programs" this is such an integral part of the program that it is even assumed that the member who doesn't do service (called "twelve-step" work) risks having a relapse. "You can't keep it," AA says, "until you give it away."

Therein lies the secret of addiction healing: one drunk talking to another. And as we see in Part 2, Chapter 6, People Ways, it's one of the surest ways to trigger a jolt cure.

CHAPTER 3

A Brief History of Jolt Recoveries

Things that are holy are revealed only to men who are holy.
　　　　　　　　—*Hippocrates, c. 460–400 B.C., Law, Book V*

HIPPOCRATES AND "THE FAVORABLE MOMENT"

Studying the history of healing is easy. There's lots written about that. But studying the history of *sudden* healing is a whole different matter. Comparatively little has been written in any kind of organized way, and what *has* been written is hard to find. What do you look under? Sudden? Spontaneous? God?

Basically, the history of instant recovery is the history of all the *obstacles* to it. As we've seen, most cultures have rejected the very idea and have dismissed the thousands of quick-cure cases we have on record as unscientific.

But the jolt-recovery phenomenon refuses to go away. "There are just too many cases of inexplicable . . . remissions and other rapid cures *not* to believe in sudden healings," claims Marilyn Ferguson, author of *The Aquarian Conspiracy.* "Both accidentally and deliberately, people have had such experiences throughout history."

From studying written records, cave drawings, and artifacts, we know that even the earliest peoples were interested in healing. Twenty-five-thousand-year-old drawings on the walls of the Lascaux caves in Southern France suggest a preoccupation with the healing arts as well as the hunt. And there's evidence from as far back as 60,000 B.C. that herbs were used as medicines. Back then, when somebody recovered from something, it was probably attributed to the medicines, to the medicine men who administered them, or perhaps to the intervention of spirit gods or magic.

On the other hand, the ancient Greeks during the age of Hippocrates, the acknowledged Father of medicine, were well aware that there was one brief moment in each case during which this healing was most likely to happen. Hippocrates called this "kairos," meaning "favorable moment."

It is, of course, during this favorable moment that the jolted-sober experience takes place. So we can say that Hippocrates was the first acknowledged supporter of this remarkable event.

THE DARK AGES IN HEALING

During the Old Testament period, starting in about 4200 B.C., an all-powerful *one*-God concept dominated the thinking of our ancestors. This replaced belief in numerous spirit gods. The culture became "sin" oriented. If you sinned, or a relative sinned, God punished you with suffering or illness. You were stuck with your sickness or misery unless He chose to forgive you by healing you through God's grace. (In Eastern thinking, of course, karma or unpaid debts from previous lifetimes might explain illnesses in this lifetime.)

Again and again throughout much of ancient history, we see how both the "cause" of illness, including afflictions such as drunkenness, and the "cure" for illness were assumed to be the result of divine intervention. Consequently, there are almost *no* stories of healers and sudden healings in the Old Testament. Why bother to try to fix something when it was God's will? Most likely this sin-and-punishment attitude also meant that people kept their illnesses a secret as long as possible to avoid public condemnation for being "bad."

A BRIGHTER VIEW

Then Christ came along. He had compassion for the afflicted and stressed a mind-body connection, meaning that he believed the individual, not just God, was partly responsible for the illness and partly responsible for the cure. Furthermore, 2,000 years before Freud, Christ stressed the importance of the powerful unconscious mind on our health.

As the result of this more holistic, humanistic view of sickness and recovery, the New Testament is full of sudden healing stories:

And going into Peter's house Jesus found Peter's mother-in-law in bed with fever. He touched her hand, and the fever left her, and she got up and began to wait on him.

—*Matthew 8:14–15*

That evening they brought him any who were possessed by devils. He cast out the spirits with a word and cured all who were sick.

—*Matthew 8:16*

These healings could certainly be described as jolt cures, triggered by the touch or mere presence of Jesus, or by some other stimuli not commented on or even recognized by those involved.

THE RETURN OF THE DARK AGES

Unfortunately, Christ's views were eclipsed soon after his death, and there was a return to the sin theory of illness that lasted for the next 15 centuries—throughout that period of time we call the Middle or Dark Ages. A glance at a book of historical timetables shows that during the Dark Ages very little went on, at least medically. Intellectual and scientific explorations were stymied. Quacks ran rampant, and alchemy flourished. There was little freedom to examine or question or disagree with the dictates of the church. Those who questioned were believed to have been prompted by witches, the evil eye, magic, or demonic possession—all stuff you didn't want to fool around with.

THE PENDULUM SWINGS

Starting with the Renaissance around 1500 A.D. came permission to question old ideas. Suddenly, scientific and intellectual exploration flourished. No longer was there danger of being put to the rack for asking how or why.

At last people began to have confidence that they could change things. People who were ill were now encouraged to take more responsibility for their conditions and play a part in their recoveries. Recovery was now in human hands.

Unfortunately, the pendulum swung too far. Suddenly too much was made of human logic and willpower. It was now assumed we had total control over our behavior—and we went at it with a vengeance.

Because the Zeitgeist, or popular world view, now said that anything new was welcome, the quacks who had been forced into secrecy during the Dark Ages began to come out of the woodwork. In France alone, 40,000 deaths a year were blamed on excessive bloodletting—a popular quack practice for curing fevers that had no scientific basis. In London, the official pharmacopeia listed nearly 2,000 drugs, including some that relied on repulsiveness for their effectiveness, such as lizard urine, rat droppings, and saliva.

But, of course, at times even these quack treatments "worked" because they served as triggers for jolt healings. Not understanding this then, any more than we seem to now, people automatically gave the credit for these cures to the last thing that happened to them just before the recoveries began: "Spider webs really work!"

But the most important thing, as Hippocrates had said so long ago, was that "favorable moment"—*timing*.

The Oriental attitude about sickness and healing was different from Western notions. They avoided assumptions about cause and effect and were more open to the idea that recovery can happen in an instant. They stressed that sick people don't have to sit around and *wait* to be struck healed or struck sober. They can *do* things (such as practice meditation) that can help bring on a jolt recovery. (More on this later.)

After the Renaissance, at least in some parts of the world, there was yet another shift back to the sin-and-punishment way of looking at illness and healing. In Europe and in the early days of America, the moralists and the Puritans revived the notion that illness was predestined by God and cure-seeking was both useless and immoral.

In the 1800s, however, reports of mass spontaneous healings, similar to those attributed to Christ, began to appear in Lourdes in Southern France and later on in Canada at St. Anne de Beaupres. These places attracted millions of visitors, a percentage of whom were healed. Of course, if millions of people go *any*where, statistically a percentage will be healed. Some stimulus or other will trigger moment-of-clarity cures. And no doubt they'll give the credit to the *place*: "Going to Lourdes really works."

Today, two million people a year still make the pilgrimage to Lourdes. I interviewed one of these visitors myself, a registered nurse in her 70s who had gone while on vacation:

> During the whole trip I'd been dogged by an eye infection and facial rash. Doctors hadn't helped. I was scheduled to visit Lourdes, just to see it. When I got there I had a thought: "If *they* can get cured, maybe *I* can do something about my eyes." So I splashed the waters on my face and in my eyes—and a few days later my eyes and rash cleared up. And to think I'd only gone to Lourdes to take a look!
>
> —*Margaret S., R.N.*

Out of the Lourdes phenomenon came religious sects, such as Christian Science, that specialized in healings. Because they value quick healings instead of scoff at them, people feel free to report them. As a result, Christian Science has offered the world thousands of valuable examples of sudden recovery.

The man who served as a bridge between the dying days of the Age of Reason and the contemporary Age of Psychology was Anton Mesmer, a physician from Austria. His theory of "Mesmerism" attributed instant healing to unseeable, astrological energy forces ("animal magnetism"). Crazy as he sounded to most of his contemporaries, he actually did have "cures" in his practice—jolt cures that he, of course, took credit for. When King Louis XV of France went to Mesmer and had a cure, he became a loyal supporter: "Mesmer's treatment really works."

Mesmerism finally faded around 1850 but is still seen as an inportant chapter in the history of sudden healing.

MODERN JOLTS

In 1902 when William James published *The Varieties of Religious Experience* and later *The Will to Believe*, he took the term *religious experience* and broadened its definition to include transformational experiences by all religions as well as by nonreligious people. Therefore, Roman Catholics, mystics, Jews, Moslems, Hindus, Buddhists, primitives, alcoholics, drug takers, atheists, neurotics, and agnostics are *all* potential candidates for "religious" or "spiritual" events. How people choose to interpret their own healing depends upon their personal orientation.

By the late 1800s and early 1900s there was, thanks to Austrian psychoanalyst Sigmund Freud, a new-found appreciation for forces *not* within our control—unconscious forces that were viewed as central in explaining a person's behavior as well as how these behaviors were cured. If a person was an alcoholic, it was because of something buried deep in the unconscious mind. To fix it you had to dig it out.

Freud was apparently suspicious of sudden healings in which this unconscious cause hadn't been determined.

Psychoanalyst Carl Jung, on the other hand, was much more open to the idea that there is something else involved in healing—something not so easily figured out. He developed the concept of the "collective unconscious." This was the view that we each have "3,000,000-year-old minds" containing all the wisdom and memories of our ancestors. Sudden healing, then, might occur when a person inadvertently taps into this universal-race wisdom for an appropriate cure. We all have within us this power to heal ourselves; our only problem has been in learning how to access it.

Abraham Maslow, another psychologist who studied transformation and sudden healing, wrote about "peak experiences," during which an individual may suddenly feel at one with the universe. Meditators work for years to achieve this at-one state. The difference between a peak experience and a jolt cure or moment-of-clarity healing is the *goal*. The goal of the peak experience is the experience itself, the good feeling. The goal of the jolt recovery is the recovery. The good feeling is an extra bonus.

Starting in the late 1930s, a psychiatrist named Harry M. Tiebout, one of the first in the medical profession to openly support Alcoholics Anonymous, wrote a series of psychiatric papers devoted to the importance of the "conversion" (moment of clarity) experience in alcoholism recovery. He defined conversion as "a psychological event in which there is a major shift in personality manifestation," and he stated that such an event was "the only thing" that could bring about the total personality change necessary for an alcoholic to maintain a lasting recovery from the illness. Unfortunately, the psychiatric field didn't listen to Tiebout, and as a result the phenomenon of spontaneous remission or instant healing in alcoholism has remained one of the best-kept secrets in the field of mental health. Only now is that beginning to change.

Even though sudden healing has always been considered something of a fluke, something of which to be a little suspicious, when you consider the large number of people who have had quick cures, it gets harder and harder not to take them seriously.

The question for us now is not *do* they happen but *how* do they happen? What causes sudden healing? Everybody's got a theory, it seems. That's what we'll look at next.

CHAPTER 4

Everybody's Got A Theory

> Science has a duty to hold a theory lightly—and let go of it joyously.
>
> *Charles Darwin*

Show me someone who's had a quick cure, and I'll show you someone with a theory about how it happened.

In this chapter we'll take a look at some of the most popular theories about what causes instant healing. There are plenty of others, but these are the ones you hear most. They fall into four categories: One, it's God; two, it's willpower; three, it's the unconscious; and four, it's biochemical.

IT'S GOD

> I woke up, and a feeling came over me. I knew it was the Lord telling me no more drinking, so I quit.
>
> —*Len, 40, sober two years*

Divine intervention is what many people believe is the "cause" of instant recovery. Christians, Jews, Moslems, and others have all agreed on this—it's the *intermediaries* who differ.

In primitive times the intermediaries were ancestral gods and spirits from the spirit world. The intermediary for

Moslems has been the prophet Mohammed; for Jews, Moses; and for Christians, the Holy Spirit or Jesus Christ.

Christ was the go-between for many of those who responded to a 1985 Gallup poll on the subject of "spiritual experiences." Four out of ten of the Americans polled claimed to have had a spiritual experience, some involving healings. Of course, when divine intervention is assumed to be the cause of a sudden healing or change, the individual is more likely to call it a religious or spiritual experience. This is how one woman explained it:

> I was very ill 15 years ago. I woke up one summer day and felt the presence of Jesus in the room [and was healed].
> —*New York housewife in Gallup poll*

In the healings below, there wasn't even a middleman involved—they came directly from God:

> By 20, I was destroyed. I had no feeling of God. But one night I got down on my knees and said, "Please show me you're here, and if you do I'll devote the rest of my life to service." Suddenly I was bathed in love, and I *knew* there was a God.
> —*Jane, 30s, sober eight years*

> I asked God what's wrong with me. Answer: "You're an alcoholic, and to recover you must go to AA." I did.
> —*B.K., 57, sober 20 years*

> One day, standing in a bean line, I looked around and said to myself, "I don't belong here. God help me out of this!" Then this guy came up to me and said, "You look bad. I know where you should go." He took me to the Salvation Army, and I've been sober ever since.
> —*Joe, 41, sober five years*

> I dropped to my knees and asked for God's help with my drinking. Then I got up and went to the hospital.
> —*Lydia, 70, sober 20 years*

God totally took away any desire to smoke. I felt nauseated at the very thought of a cigarette.

—*Claire, 40, cigarette-free 16 years*

I'd smoked for 30 years. One day the Lord said, "It's time to quit." I said "I can't do it." The Lord said, "It's time to quit." I said "okay," and I felt a great peace and the presence of the Holy Spirit within me. I haven't smoked since.

—*Nadine, 58, cigarette-free 10 years*

IT'S WILLPOWER

For many people saying "God did it" isn't a satisfying answer. Perhaps it *should* be, but it's not—maybe because they are atheists or agnostics or maybe just because, as an answer, it strikes them as intellectually lazy.

At least half of the original members of Alcoholics Anonymous considered themselves agnostics, which led co-founder Bill Wilson to write a special chapter in the book *Alcoholics Anonymous* called "We Agnostics," the purpose of which was to reassure agnostics that it isn't necessary to believe in "God" to recover from alcoholism. A generic-type spiritual or moment-of-clarity experience will do just as well.

I had a moment of clarity when I suddenly looked at my life and all the pills I was taking and said, "I'm only 19. How come I'm afraid to go outside? How come I have all these fears? What's wrong with me?" I went for treatment, and I've been clean and sober ever since.

—*Denise, 23, sober four years*

I made a conscious decision to get well.

—*Nancy, 52, sober nine years*

One day I just lay down and stopped.

—*Man calling in to a radio talk show on addiction*

I just made up my mind *not* to drink. I said to myself, "I just don't want it."

—*Menlo, 53, sober two years*

The willpower theory of recovery is the point of view that everything going on in the brain is conscious and rational, a theory first made popular during the Age of Reason, and that if we really "buckle down" and "set our minds to it" we can overcome addiction. When willpower enthusiasts have a jolt recovery, they usually take the credit for it by constructing a chain of logical steps about how they got from here to there. Or, "I just decided that's it, enough!" they'll say. After all, that's what the experience feels like to them.

Back in the 1930s my father had TB. Those were the days when we didn't have spontaneous remissions. If you did, you didn't talk about it. Anyway, my father's doctor told him he was terminal. In the hospital, a friend of his came to visit and said, "You know, Sid, you don't have to just lie there and die. You can fight this thing. Your mind is the strongest force in this whole universe." The next day my father's fever broke, and he recovered. Today he just tosses the whole incident off as if it were nothing. "It's just mind over matter," is all he'll say about it.

—*D. S., 40s, herself sober 13 years*

IT'S THE UNCONSCIOUS

It's not the mental mind that solves problems overnight but the higher mind.

—*Robert Louis Stevenson*

There is no doubt of the necessary intervention of some previous mental process unknown to the inventor—in other terms, an unconscious one.

—*Jacques Hadamard, mathematician*

Another common explanation for sudden healing is the unconscious mind, that part of the human psyche that lies beyond consciousness, beyond willpower. Though Sigmund Freud usually gets the credit for discovering the unconscious, he himself said that all he did was discover a scientific way to study it but that the unconscious itself had already been discovered by poets and philosophers. In the Bible the word *heart* is often used to mean the unknown (unconscious) inner self and not the organ. "As a man thinketh in his heart, so he is." When Martin Luther had his "lightning bolt" spiritual experience, it was, according to one writer, James Loder, in his book *The Transforming Moment*, "a bolt—not just from the heavens above, but also from the psyche beneath." It came from his unconscious.

During all those centuries when the focus was on willpower and consciousness, the unconscious was sorely neglected. People were even scared of it and saw it as something mysterious that they couldn't see or control.

Philosopher William James believed that there was a reason that people assumed healings came from God instead of from within:

> [It] is one of the peculiarities of invasions from the subconscious region to take on objective appearances, and to suggest to the subject an external control. In the religious life the control is felt as "higher."
>
> —*William James in* The Will to Believe

This may be why so many people who have had moment-of-clarity healings, even those who don't believe in God, still don't feel as though they did it themselves. Some speak of "another voice" that's *not* their own:

> I didn't have a clue that I was an alcoholic. One day I heard an outside voice. It wasn't a thought, it was a voice that was *not* self-generated. It said, "You're an alcoholic." It said it three times. I went right to AA, and I've been sober ever since. A few years later the same thing happened with smoking. I was thinking, "Maybe I'll wait until tomorrow to quit; it's St. Patrick's Day, it's memorable." Then that voice said, "No, do it today. Stop today." And I

stopped that day. In each case, stopping cold like that, I expected to be uncomfortable—but I wasn't.

—*C. J., 40s, sober 14 years, cigarette-free 10 years*

This is how the book, *Alcoholics Anonymous*, explains it: "With few exceptions, our members find that they tap an un-suspected inner resource." Many, of course, interpret this as meaning the unconscious mind.

IT'S BIOCHEMICAL

The brain is no simple instrument. It contains anywhere from 10 billion to 100 billion neurons—cells with long strands called dendrites—which reach out to touch other neurons. According to the *Newsweek* cover story called "How The Brain Works" (February 7, 1983), there are up to one quadrillion of these neural connections. The brain also contains more than 50 chemicals (with more being discovered all the time) called neurotransmitters, which are chemical substances that carry messages throughout the mind via the neurons.

Any number of things can trigger the release of neuro-transmitters, from emotions to artificial stimulation with elec-trodes to ingesting food. Tryptophan, for example, found in many foods including bananas, when ingested becomes the neurotransmitter serotonin, which is related to, among other things, appetite. Eggs, soybeans, and liver trigger a neuro-transmitter that helps make new memories. A third neuro-transmitter is related to blood pressure and depression. According to the article, "the best way to incorporate food into the mind remains untested, but the next generation of mind drugs just might come from the refrigerator."

The endorphins, which we hear a lot about, are the natural opiate-like substances that scientists assume can also be found in the brain. When stimulated by such things as exercise or acupuncture, they are released and function both to kill pain and to make us feel good emotionally—which is why they're often called the "feel-good" chemicals. One of the bad things that happens to drug takers is the fact that when they're taking the drugs (like morphine and cocaine), the neurons are flooded with so many artificial opiates that the brain stops producing the natural opiates (endorphins). Then, when the addict goes for treatment and tries to get clean and sober, he's miserable because now he has neither the artificial nor the natural "feel-good" chemicals. In cases like this, detox and early sobriety are definitely a "feel-bad" experience. It can take weeks for the brain to resume normal production of the natural opiates—if the recovering addict is lucky. I've heard some experts speculate that in some cases, the addict does such damage to the brain that he or she may have ruined the production of endorphins for good. Perhaps this is why we're seeing that cocaine is one of the hardest drugs to stay off of; the "happy" chemicals are never replaced.

> I just couldn't get together. I wanted to stay clean and sober, but I just couldn't get myself to care about anything, not even who won the World Series. Everybody kept saying, "Hang in there—it gets better," but it didn't. It was all gray all the time and it stayed gray. Finally, I said, "If this is sobriety, who needs it," and I went back to using cocaine.
>
> —*Felix, 20s, still using cocaine*

In cases where there hasn't been interference, as there was in Felix's case, the messages that travel around the brain are also sent out to the body, to the muscles, organs, fats, and enzymes, and appear to affect what happens there.

The notion that the brain can affect the body goes back thousands of years. Medicine men everywhere have known it. And in many Eastern traditions, the mind/body connection is considered basic medicine. Even to the most casual observer this is blatantly obvious. All you have to do is think about sucking a lemon, and you know immediately it's true: Your mouth puckers.

But 300 years ago French philosopher René Descartes put forth his theory of dualism, which separates mind and body:

"What's mental is mental; what's physical is physical." Dualism has had a great influence on our thinking and on mainstream Western medicine ever since, closing our minds to any kind of holistic view of healing.

New discoveries are revealing once again that emotions and attitudes can affect us right down to the cells of our immune system and vice versa, creating a kind of "feedback loop." The brain sends chemicals to the immune system and the immune system in turn sends chemicals back to the brain. Sometimes these chemical changes can actually trigger a jolt healing.

An article in the *Los Angeles Times* (September 18, 1988) and a cover story in the November 11, 1988, issue of *Newsweek* called "Body and Soul," describe a new (decade old) science called psychoneuroimmunology (PNI), which has neuroscientists, immunologists, psychologists, psychiatrists, and others investigating in a cooperative way (perhaps for the first time) to better understand the mind/body connection—the complex interactions between the central nervous system (brain) and the body's immune system. According to *Newsweek*, they are trying to rejoin what some feel should "never have been put asunder." Like Humpty-Dumpty, they are trying to put body and soul back together again.

The immune system, which the *Times* article referred to as "really our 6th sense," is almost as complex as the brain. It consists of a vast array of specialty cells that dwell in the thymus gland, spleen, bone marrow, and lymph nodes. It also keeps watch over our bloodstream. When threatened, the cells attack by producing antibodies. Once in a while the immune system overdoes it and sends out a whole army of attack cells against an invading ant bite or bee sting. The well-known "allergic" reaction of swelling and itching is the result.

In *Anatomy of an Illness*, Norman Cousins claims that for the most part, our body's built-in mechanisms to resist illness are so effective and subtle that most of the time when a disease like cancer starts, the body automatically and successfully challenges it, and we're not even aware that we've had a spontaneous recovery or remission.

In his book, Cousins cites Nobel Prize winner, Dr. Albert Schweitzer, the famous physician, theologian, and African missionary, who often said that each patient carries his or her own doctor inside and that it is our job as patients and as healers to let that "inner physician," the brain and the immune system, go to work.

With this compelling evidence for a mind/body connection, it is not surprising to read, as I did a few years ago in *Psychology Today*, that even compulsive gambling, which we've always thought of as a purely psychological illness, may have a physiological component. Perhaps gambling triggers (in some people) production of the feel-good endorphins, and the gambler, to keep feeling good, keeps gambling. There's no proof of this yet, but it's interesting to speculate about.

Which of these four theories explains how a jolt recovery happens? Is it God? Is it willpower? Is it the unconscious? Or is it biochemical? We just don't know yet. All we do know is that a good theory should not only explain jolt healings but should also help us predict when they'll happen again. So far, none of these theories can do this.

But even though we can't explain or predict jolt cures or *make* them happen, we can at least take some actions that will greatly increase our chances of successful recovery.

So let's take a look at what these are.

PART 2

SEVEN WAYS
TO ROMANCE
A JOLT RECOVERY

CHAPTER 5

Selecting Your Romance Method

All who take this remedy recover in a short time except those whom it does not help, who all die and have no relief from other medicine. Therefore, it is obvious that it fails only in incurable cases.
—*Galen, ancient Greek physician*

STARTING THE FIRE

What can you do to make a jolt recovery happen to you or to another person?

This may well turn out to be *the* question in the decade ahead because what we're doing now to fight addiction isn't working. A less than 10 percent "cure" rate isn't good enough.

At present, nobody knows enough to guarantee you a moment-of-clarity healing. At the same time, you don't have to sit out on your back porch in a rocking chair and wait to be struck sober. That's like waiting for lightning to strike and start a fire so you can cook dinner.

Romancing a jolt cure means adding something, picking out one or more of the seven suggested romance methods, all of which are calculated to trigger instant cures, and then doing something about it. There are probably as many ways to be jolted sober as there are addicted people. The divisions here are just for convenience, but there will no doubt be some overlap as well as some things that get left out. I find these seven categories useful and trust you will, too. For example, I've learned that, for me at least, the first method (People Ways)

41

is usually the most effective. Whatever my problem is, I start
there.

GETTING TRIGGER-HAPPY

As you read the seven chapters, keep in mind that what you're
ultimately looking for isn't "the best treatment for addiction"
but the treatment or activity with the best "trigger potential,"
which is a very different thing. Aim at the thing most likely to
trigger your jolt cure.

Earlier I said that I've observed there are actually *two* phases
of the addiction-recovery process—the pre-jolt phase and the
post-jolt phase. In the pre-jolt phase, even if the person has
stopped drinking, drugging, eating, or gambling, the obsession
(which *is* the addiction) may still be operating, so the addicted
person has a hard time. It's a fight. AA calls it white-knuckle
sobriety, and it's during this phase that there are frequent relapses. In the post-jolt phase the obsession disappears, for
whatever reasons, and the fight is over. In this phase "Just Say
No" comes easy.

It's obviously this phase in which you want to be. Here's a
good example of the shift from the pre-jolt to the post-jolt
phase:

> I tried to quit drinking once or twice before, but it was hard, and I
> couldn't. Then one day I tried again—and it wasn't hard at all. I
> haven't had a drink in over two years.
> —actor *George C. Scott on* Good Morning America

The focus here is on *triggers*, not treatments. Therefore, Part
2 is neither a referral directory nor an analysis of existing
treatments. There are already plenty of books that do that job
quite well. When I mention existing treatments or groups, it's
because every single one of them, good and bad, contains ele-
ments that can trigger a jolt cure.

Which romance method is for you? Let's look at them one
by one.

CHAPTER 6

People Ways

> I heard a woman speak at an AA meeting about her life, and it changed my life.
> —*Janet, 29, sober two years*

PUT YOUR BODY WHERE THEY'RE TALKING ABOUT YOUR PROBLEM

When you have a problem or you're upset, what's your first impulse? For many people it's the impulse to *talk* to somebody: to call a friend, make an appointment with a therapist or counselor, visit a neighbor, share it with a stranger—even a bartender.

People have always sought each other out for the purpose of healing, so there must be something to it. Most cultures hold the idea that the ill are best healed, not by being isolated, but by being surrounded by other people. The current explosion of self-help, therapy, human-potential, and consciousness-raising groups isn't new. It's a rediscovery of an ancient wisdom: People need people. Today there's a support group for just about every ailment. The very foundation of Alcoholics Anonymous, the granddaddy of all addiction-based support groups, is "one drunk talking to another." We hear somebody make a comment, we share a secret, it triggers a shift within, and we're never the same again.

43

Why does it work? Probably because we're *made* to change. People aren't rocks. People have permeable boundaries so we can let in new information. Sometimes this new information acts as a trigger and ends up changing us, or being the catalyst for a jolt cure. People who resist letting in new information are even described in rocklike terms: "It's like talking to a wall"; "He's so closed off"; "She's so hardheaded."

Because we're social creatures, we're vulnerable to social pressure. We care what other people think, even though we like to believe we're independent and know our own minds. But being susceptible to social pressure isn't all bad. It can help save our lives if it pushes at us to do constructive, instead of destructive, things. AA says "Stick with the winners." What this means is that if you associate with people whose values you'd like to have, even if you don't have those values now, they'll rub off on you. If you want to be sober or thin or stop smoking or gambling, hang out with people who are sober or thin or don't smoke or gamble, and after a while you'll "catch" it.

In self-help groups a kind of paradigm shift takes place. The group consciousness that says "addiction is bad" draws the newcomer into it—and suddenly the newcomer thinks addiction is bad, also. This in itself can trigger a jolt cure. (So make sure the group you pick has a healthy, not a toxic, consciousness.) When you go to a meeting of AA and sit down, for example, you're like a giant TV satellite dish taking in all kinds of information. Sooner or later you are bound to pick up a channel that will trigger a jolt cure. It's practically inevitable.

WE'RE ALL IN THIS TOGETHER

Long, long ago before overpopulation and industrialization, each individual's contribution to the community was necessary in order to make the community work. In that context, any kind of illness was a great threat to the whole. If it happened, everybody jumped in and helped out so they could get the sick person functioning again as soon as possible. Sometimes this meant taking over the sick person's job, or bringing over antelope soup, or praying for recovery, or providing child care. The illness belonged to everybody: everybody had a stake in it; everybody had a hand in curing it.

Today this isn't so—at least not in most places. But it still exists in many of the anonymous self-help groups. The illness of each member is seen as affecting the whole; helping the newcomer is considered everyone's responsibility.

It's too bad that for so many years we got away from group-healing concepts. We went along with Freud and others who insisted on isolating the patient from relatives and the environment. That's how I was trained. As a therapist, I felt disloyal to a patient if I so much as chatted with a relative on the phone. But isolating a patient makes sense only if his or her environment is negative. For example, a drug addict's junkie friends certainly aren't good for him. But it doesn't make sense to pull somebody away from a supportive family. The more *people* the better.

The support as well as the peer pressure in the anonymous groups helps the addicted person curb the addictive behavior, even in the pre-jolt phase. There's definite improvement along the way, even if there are slips. The sharing of "experience, strength and hope," as AA puts it, is healing in itself. One typical reaction to walking into an anonymous group meeting for the first time is: "It's such a relief to realize I'm not alone!"

The fact that we have expressions in our culture such as "God works through people" is further evidence that our ultimate answers will come from each other. The late Indian mystic and philosopher mentioned earlier, Swami Muktananda, after spending 25 years searching all over India for God, finally found his spiritual awakening one day when he looked in his own guru's eyes. For him, this moment of initiation (his terminology for the moment-of-clarity event) was "more important than all the years of training and experience" that preceded it.

The upshot of all this is that if you're suffering from an addiction, the best way to beat it, even if you insist on continuing to practice it, is to put your body where they're talking about your primary problem—meaning, go to some kind of meeting, group, or class. Go where there are lots of other people. This is better by far, I think, than seeing a psychotherapist or counselor one to one, although sometimes this kind of people contact can help prompt the addicted person to go to a self-help group—that is, if the therapist knows about addiction and self-help groups. Unfortunately, too many don't.

In groups, remember what you're ultimately there for is that precious *trigger*, and obviously a room full of people talking about addiction—*your* addiction—has more trigger potential for you than sitting in your living room or your therapist's office. Sometimes people are jolted sober sitting at home, but why not up the odds?

So keep it simple. Find out where there's some kind of meeting, lecture, seminar, or workshop where people will be talking out loud about your *primary* addiction (you can handle your other addictions later, if you have them). Then go there, sit down, and listen.

That may be all you have to do! That's all I did, and because I did it I've been sober for more than sixteen years. And it hasn't been hard, at least not so far.

If you look at going to a self-help group meeting as just walking into a place, sitting down for an hour or an hour and a half, and listening—then it's not that big a deal, right? It's not like Turning Yourself In. You don't even have to tell anybody you're going. You can go to Alcoholics Anonymous, Cocaine Anonymous (CA), Smokers Anonymous (SA), Narcotics Anonymous (NA), Overeaters Anonymous (OA), Gamblers Anonymous (GA)—or any of the other helping groups such as Smoke Enders and Weight Watchers (even though there's a charge for some) just the way you'd stop in and see a movie on your way home from work. If you don't like it, you can leave and go back another time, or go to a meeting in another location. They are all different.

DEPOSIT THOSE SILVER DOLLARS

The anonymous groups understand that not everybody loves being there. Usually people end up liking it a lot. And each time you go it's another couple of silver dollars in your slot machine. The speaker says something, a coin drops in. The guy behind you says something, another coin drops in. The woman next to you gives you her phone number, another coin drops in. You remember something, another coin drops in. During the week that follows, you think of somebody's face from the meeting. Yet another coin drops in. Then one day, when you least expect it, the last coin drops in, and you hit the jackpot and have your jolt cure.

What if you've already been to lots of meetings and it still doesn't "work"? Don't despair. If you put coins in a slot machine and didn't hit the jackpot, would you say the slot machine doesn't "work"? Of course not, because you know it's a question of timing. Well, it's a question of timing with addiction recovery, too.

However, when the timing is right, even something totally ridiculous can trigger a jolt cure:

> I was listening to a speaker at an AA meeting. She talked about how all her life she'd looked for the Great Big Ice Cream Cone in the Sky, and when she said that, I *knew* that was me! I'd done that! And I've been sober ever since.
>
> —*Marlena, 50, sober 15 years*

Now who would have predicted that a remark about the Great Big Ice Cream Cone in the Sky would have been this woman's turning point? Nobody, least of all Marlena. The lesson here is: Don't predict, just go!

If at this point you're howling, "I'm not a joiner!" or "I hate groups!" then welcome to the club. Probably most of the millions of people who make up the various self-help addiction groups hate groups. Members like to call AA "the biggest loner's club in the world." Still, they go, and they get better anyway.

A DIRECTORY OF SORTS

Okay, so *where* do you go? Since this isn't a referral directory, finding out where you can put your body to hear them talk about your primary problem will be up to you. But in general the most obvious answer is one of the community self-help groups. I'm always amazed when I hear people complain that there's not enough treatment for addiction, as co-host Jane Pauley did on the "Today Show" when she said, after viewing a film clip on Narcotics Anonymous, "yes, but *real* treatment costs money." Well, self-help groups *are* "real" treatment, and they're ubiquitous; they're everywhere. By the latest count, there are over 150 self-help groups that are based on the AA twelve-step model. Like cell division, these groups multiply constantly to fill the expanding need. Someday there may be more people *in* self-help groups than out.

There are variations on the names of some of these groups in different parts of the country. You can get their numbers from Information, and then call and ask questions. Just remember not to judge any group or organization by one meeting. You wouldn't judge all movies by *one* movie, would you? Go to at least 10 or 20 before coming to any conclusions. Go back to the ones you like, and skip the ones you don't (if you have the luxury of many to choose from where you live). Make it as pleasant as possible for yourself: you'll be more open to your jolt cure that way.

In some places people with cocaine problems go to AA instead of CA, which is relatively new and doesn't yet exist in many areas. AA is full of people whose primary drug is something else, so don't be fooled by the title of the group. You can have a jolt cure even if you're at the wrong meeting! If for some reason you don't want to start with an anonymous group, or you need something a little more intense, consider an inpatient treatment program; there are between 7,000 and 10,000 of them nationwide for chemical dependency plus there are now an increasing number of eating-disorder units. If you have the time (three or four weeks), the money ($8,000 and up), and/or the insurance (some plans cover this), then an inpatient treatment program is great—a real crash course on the subject of addiction. You'll get intensely "peopled" there, what with therapy groups, discussion groups, lectures, counseling, and visits to appropriate anonymous groups. It's wonderful. And sometimes the jolt cure comes at 3 in the morning when patients, unable to sleep, sit huddled together talking in the day room or near the nurses' station.

There are also outpatient programs, day programs, and programs for people who have to keep on working. New programs are being developed all the time.

If you're after something less intense, check the Yellow Pages. Look up the name of your addiction and see what's listed. You might be surprised at just how *much* is available. Check to see if there are information and referral phone numbers and call them. For drugs and alcohol, there's the National Council on Alcoholism, which has 200 affiliates. For overeaters there are all kinds of programs. Weight Watchers and OA are the biggest and best known. They have meetings nationwide. And don't forget to check local newspapers for seminars and classes. I've been a Rotary speaker on addiction, a seminar speaker, a workshop speaker, an adult-education-class speaker, a church speaker. Others like me are doing the same thing all over town. Go listen. Any one of those speakers could be your key to a jolt cure.

Here's what happened to one young woman who dropped in to hear a talk on addiction at her local library:

> My moment of clarity came one Tuesday night at the library, when I heard a psychologist talk about the nature of addiction. It gave me the courage to sign myself into a halfway house for alcoholic women. I lived there clean and sober for a year. Now I'm out, and I'm fine.
>
> —*Estelle, 29, sober 13 months*

You just never know!

CHAPTER 7

Physical Ways

The great aim in life is not knowledge but action.
—*Thomas Huxley*

Change is movement, being in action.
—*Andrew Weil*, The Natural Mind

YOUR LEGS ARE THE WHEELS OF THOUGHT

If your natural instinct when you're upset is to go ride a bike or take a hike instead of getting on the phone and talking to a friend, then that could be your body telling you something. Listen to that "inner physician" who Albert Schweitzer talked about. Consider the possibility that, for *you* at least, the quickest way to your health is through your muscles. You may just have to get physical.

Some people seem to be born more physical than others. Where one person will try to solve a problem by taking a workshop or curling up on the couch, another will get up and pace the floor. Legend has it that Einstein went sailing when he was stuck on a mathematical problem. Sometimes, as he stared up at the clouds or out over the waves, the answer he'd been looking for would suddenly pop into his mind, fully formed. All that was left was to go back to his desk and fill in the steps in between. (Another version of this story says that Einstein once came up with a winning formula when he went out for ice cream, which leads me to think that there might be something after all to that Big Ice Cream Cone in the Sky story in the previous chapter!) Many sports professionals have described peak or transformational experiences while chasing a ball.

WASHING CUPS AND OTHER SPORTS

Over the course of the fifteen years I've worked in chemical dependency, I've heard many recovering addicts and alcoholics say that their turning-point moment came while they were doing something physical—running on the beach, washing the kitchen floor, doing aerobics. When old-timer AA members tell alcoholics the way to stay sober is clean up the meeting hall and wash cups, they're saying the same thing: Do something physical, and your answers will come. When so many addiction-recovery stories have the same punchline, there has to be something to it.

Action people sometimes need action cures. If they're going to be struck sober, it's more likely to happen playing ball than playing chess or hearing a lecturer. For them, "treatment" may mean "play." Their list of potential jolt-cure triggers is endless: running, basketball, swimming, mountaineering, hiking, wilderness treks, fishing, tennis, wrestling, soccer, baseball, walking, football, dancing, aerobics, golf, martial arts, body-building, bodywork therapies, travel, assembly lines, everyday chores such as housework and commuting—even Disneyland. Being in action jiggles loose whatever insightful nugget of information it is they need to heal themselves. This isn't a scientific explanation, of course, but I think it helps to visualize it this way. Maybe activity stirs up those feel-good endorphins, or perhaps the increase of oxygen to the brain does something. Whatever it is, if you're the physical type, you should consider this as part of your personalized treatment plan.

One Runner's Story

Years ago I cut an article called "Running Away from Alcoholism" out of *Running Times*, a newspaper. It was about a recovered-alcoholic marathon runner. He'd started running when he was still drinking. Even with a hangover, he'd get out there and run. According to the article, "one day he just stopped drinking." Four years later (when the interview in the article took place), he was still mystified about how it had happened. In fact, he was so fearful he'd lose it that he joined AA to maintain it. (As we see later in Chapter 13, "Maintaining Your Jolt Recovery," this was a smart move.)

Of course, knowing what we know, I think it's safe to say that what happened to our marathon runner was a jolt cure. And running triggered it.

He didn't know that he was intuitively romancing a jolt cure when he took up running, but that's what happened. Fortunately for him, his instincts were right on. Despite hangovers, his "inner doctor" knew what he had to do. Survival instincts were at work.

Many of us have an inner instinct about what to do to heal ourselves. The trouble is we don't always heed it. We push it away—like Marco did, as you're about to read.

Marco

Marco was a patient in the chemical-dependency treatment center in which I work. He was a "retread." He'd been in our unit before, four or five times. He'd stay sober for a while (biting the bullet), and then he'd drink again. This time he felt humiliated. He sat there in group, hunched over, a hangdog look on his face. He'd done *everything* he'd been told to do, he said. He'd stepped up his AA meetings, he'd gotten a sponsor, he was "working the steps," he was helping others. But he'd slipped anyway.

Somehow during the course of this discussion we got sidetracked onto sports (not hard to do with a dozen young guys in the group). Marco began telling us about squash, how he loved playing squash. You could tell he loved it just by the way he lit up when talking about it. "I feel good when I'm playing squash," he said. "It's the only time I don't worry about my drinking." Then he added, visibly sinking down in his seat, "The trouble is with all these extra AA meetings I have to go to, I don't have any time for squash." It was at this point that I made an obvious suggestion: "When you leave here, Marco, how about a little more squash and a little less AA?"

At first he looked shocked, as if what I'd just said was blasphemy. But then he looked relieved—here was permission to play squash without guilt. "Yeah, you're right," he said. "That's what I'm going to do!"

That was more than five years ago, and I'd love to tell you that Marco went out and played squash and is still sober today, but I don't know if that's true. All I know is that if he slipped again, he didn't come back to our hospital—so I can just hope he's fine. The point is, there are lots of Marcos out there. *You* may be a Marco. And what he taught me was that anything that works is treatment. If you have a hunch that playing hopscotch will boost your trigger potential, then play hopscotch.

THE LAST ONE PERCENT

As a note of caution here, let me add that I'm not suggesting you skip your anonymous group or Weight Watchers meetings and play horseshoes instead. Far from it. I'm suggesting you *add* horseshoes. There's so much evidence that people contact is the most likely jolt-cure trigger for many people, it wouldn't make sense to drop it. There's nothing that says you can't do two or more romance methods at one time—the buckshot approach. That's the approach most treatment centers instinctively use, so you might as well do it, too. In Heinz's case, it's hard to tell which stimulus did the trick—physical exercise, humiliation, or sleep:

> I was in high school. I was All-State in five sports. I was written up in the *Los Angeles Times* as Athlete of the Month several times. In 1972, I was named Outstanding Teenager of America. Still, I

drank, took pills, and smoked hash. On the day of our Senior graduation rehearsal, I showed up drunk. Suddenly the Vice Principal picked up his bullhorn: "Heinz, are you graduating with us, or are you just going to stay here in school and fool around?" When I heard that it was like time stood still. I was humiliated in front of 3000 people. But at that precise moment I realized how I was destroying my life. That afternoon I went home and took a nap, and when I woke up I just decided to change. From that moment on I've been sober and drug free.

—Heinz, 36, sober 17 years

Again, remember your goal, which is that precious trigger. That's the ball to keep your eye on. Sure, improvement and progress along the way is wonderful. You can go on for years like that. But "improvement" will only take you 99 percent of the way. For that last 1 percent you need a jolt cure.

THE GENTLE NUDGE

Getting physical doesn't always mean heavy-duty exercise. Here's the case of a physician who was both an alcoholic and a compulsive overeater. His two-and-a-half-year jolt recovery from *both* addictions was triggered by getting an exercise bike:

I got on this exercise bike and found that I actually enjoyed it. I kept adjusting it to make it harder and harder. I rode it every day, and at the end of 25 or 30 minutes I'd feel good. My depression lifted, I began to eat better, and then one day when I was on the bike I suddenly realized that I wanted to stay sober. I stopped drinking, and it wasn't even hard. I stayed sober for two and a half years. But then what happened was I got busy in my life and stopped riding the bike. I began to eat junk food and get depressed again and eventually, to handle the depression, I drank.

—Elliot, 40s, still not sober and back in hospital

For this physician to heal himself again the logical prescription is: Get back on the bike! It's amazing that not once during his three-year relapse did he think of that. Hopefully now that he's recalled what worked before, he'll try it again.

Another "sport" for those who aren't strenuous physical types is walking. Many addiction-recovery programs recommend this. It burns calories, it's good for digestion, circulation, and mood—and it increases the likelihood of a jolt cure, which is the part in which we're most interested. Once that happens, the rest of whatever program it is is easy.

SHOWER POWER

It may be stretching it to say that stepping into a shower is exercise, but it is a physical action that works for a surprising number of people. My computer-programmer husband swears by showers for creativity. When he wants an answer from his unconscious mind for a tricky problem—into the shower he goes. He lets that hot water hit the back of his head, and sooner or later one of those buried nuggets of truth melts loose and gives him his solution.

It's been the trigger for some addiction recoveries, too:

> I'd been drinking myself to death, but I was still in denial about it. One morning, as I was stepping into the shower, I *knew* I'd never have to drink again. I was so excited about this, I could hardly wait to get out of the shower and begin my new life.
>
> —*Jack, 44, sober seven years*

AUTO POWER

Driving a car, another nonstrenuous "sport," has also worked for some:

> I was a musician for seventeen years. I'd leave one place and drive 1,500 miles, only stopping for gas. After the first twelve hours, the music would get boring. After the next twelve, the talk shows would get boring. Finally I'd turn the radio off, and then all I'd have was the dark highway and my own thoughts. That's when I got to know myself and was able to make two major decisions: to stop cocaine and to stop smoking. I did both.
>
> —*Ramon, 44, sober 13 years, cigarette-free 12 years*

Sometimes it's not the physical activity itself so much as what's going on in the environment in which you're doing the activity that triggers a jolt cure. Below is the case of a newly sober alcoholic, still in the pre-jolt phase, when he decided to take a stroll down a busy street and saw an accident. It triggered his moment of clarity:

> I stood there at least 45 minutes watching as the firemen, the police, the insurance investigator, and then the tow-truck operator all approached the drivers of the cars involved and asked them questions. All I could think was: "What if that was *me*, and I had alcohol on my breath?" I used to drink beer in the car on my way home from work all the time. I remember saying to myself, "I'm never going to do that again."
>
> —*Harry, 28, sober one month*

TRUST YOUR INNER SPORTS DOCTOR

If you're addicted to something—person, place, substance, or activity—you probably know that you should be "good" and go to a self-help group meeting every day. But what if your soul is screaming, "Tennis! Tennis!"? Well, go play tennis. *Then* go to the AA meeting. Let your inner sports doctor lead the way.

Some of you may say, "Well, I've been doing X, Y, or Z exercise for *years* and never had a moment-of-clarity experience about anything while doing it." That may be true. The difference is, *now* you'll be doing it consciously, which will help you hang in there when otherwise you might quit—like Marco—because you don't have time.

If your inner sports doc says "run for your life," then trust him—and *make* time.

CHAPTER 8

Intellectual Ways

I read in this news magazine that alcoholism is a disease and not a moral issue, and it changed my whole life.
> —*Connie, 30, sober two years*

My doctor gave me a pamphlet on how drinking damages the liver, and I read it and haven't had a drink since.
> —*Ed, 57, sober four years*

In my anger, I threw the book on my bed. Then my eyes focused on one sentence in the book: "We cannot live with anger." Suddenly I was on my knees. Outside the grass looked greener, everything seemed to sing. For the first time I felt free.
> —*Marty Mann, first woman to get permanently sober in AA (in 1939 at age 35) and founder of the National Council on Alcoholism (NCA)*

READ ALL ABOUT IT

A few years after I got sober, I wrote an article about my drinking and recovery experiences and sold it to *Ms.* magazine. A couple of months after the article was published, I spoke at a recovery-group meeting. I related my story. Afterward a woman came up to me. "You're the reason I'm here," she said.

"I read your article and realized I was an alcoholic. I turned myself in, and I've been sober six weeks."

I was flabbergasted. When I was out there drinking, I *never* would have read an article on alcoholism. Are you kidding? I didn't want to know the truth. Whenever I saw the word *alcoholism* in a magazine, I flipped the page. I know it sounds funny for a writer to be saying this, but for me the written word has the *least* jolt-cure potential. I love reading, but when it comes to the important things in life, I want to hear about it, not read about it. I want it to come from people. I once found myself on a river raft going down the rapids of the Colorado just because somebody had talked to me about it at a party! Now, I'd *read* about white-water rafting lots of times, but the first time somebody told me about it, I had to do it.

But there are people who are just the opposite, information junkies who cling to the written word like I did to my orange life preserver on that raft. There are people who'd simply rather read all about it than hear all about it. They can be reading along and all of a sudden some fact will jump off the page and change them forever, like the two examples at the beginning of this chapter.

THOSE FABULOUS FACTS

If you're one of these information junkies, you couldn't be living in a better time—the Information Age. We're surrounded with facts, more than most of us could ever hope to or even want to know. And now you can even make reading a book, seeing a movie, collecting pamphlets, looking in a dictionary, glancing at a cereal box, or listening to talk radio a legitimate part of your Personal Addiction-Treatment Plan, because now you know that anything that works is treatment and that sometimes facts work to trigger jolt cures. Here's a compulsive money-spender who finally found her fatal fact:

> Nothing helped my compulsive spending—no therapy, no insight, no nothing, until one day I read in a newspaper article that getting

rid of money is the same thing as getting rid of power. I said to myself, "I'll never spend money that way again!" And I haven't.
—*Barbara, 51, free from compulsive spending, five years*

When I got sober back in the early 1970s you could hardly find a book on alcoholism. Now they're everywhere, and on every other addiction as well. Back then, magazine articles on addiction were rare. Now they make the covers. A radio or TV show dealing with chemical dependency was a unique event. Now they boost ratings. I remember I had a difficult time trying to sell that article I finally sold to *Ms*. One very famous women's magazine turned it down "because we carry too many liquor ads."

So take advantage of this addiction-information glut we're now enjoying. Here's your chance to approach your addiction as if it were a term paper you had to research. Read all about it—it just may provide you with the trigger you need to be jolted sober.

Go to the magazine stand. Go to the library. Go to the bookstores. Some of them have entire sections devoted to addictions. In fact, in some cities there are even addiction bookstores. Also, you can subscribe to addiction newspapers, addiction magazines, addiction journals. You can even get T-shirts and bumper stickers, jewelry and greeting cards: "Congratulations on your first AA birthday!" Turn on the TV and, guess what, an addiction special or a made-for-TV movie with an addiction theme. Even Hollywood has gotten on the addiction bandwagon. And for you computer hackers, there's even a recovery "bulletin board" you can call in to with your modem.

HEALING BY THE BOOK

With all that is available now, there's bound to be some delicious little fact, statistic, or point of information that can turn your head. All along there have always been people who got jolted sober by the written word. Here's what a physician who now works in the chemical-dependency field told me about himself:

> I had been trying to quit smoking for years. While taking a special course in psychiatry, we were handed a book written by an internationally known layman. Most of the physicians in the group did not read the book. I decided to read it and found therein the statement that gave me a profound moment of clarity: "What the mind can conceive and believe, the mind can achieve." At this moment I was able to conceive of myself as a "nonsmoker" and believe it. That was 24 years ago and from that moment to this I have not returned to this powerful addiction.
>
> —*James West, M.D., former medical director of the Betty Ford Center*

The next case is a man who picked up the book *Alcoholics Anonymous* specifically to devalue it:

> But when I got to page 21 and read the words "the alcoholic is seldom mildly intoxicated. He is always more or less insanely drunk," I knew that was me and the jig was up.
>
> —*Jack K., 58, sober 18 years*

Here's a woman whose addiction to a person, her alcoholic husband, was "cured" as the result of reading some words in a book:

> While reading a book called *Co-Dependent No More* I realized for the first time that I had a choice about whether or not to put up with the pain of being married to an addict. I decided to stay in the marriage but to detach myself. This gave me a sense of great release, and it totally took away the anguish of my situation.
>
> —*Francis, age 31*

In the following case, a man got something other than a "fact" out of what he read:

> Because I was a cocaine addict I didn't identify with the alcoholics I heard speak at AA meetings. But I decided to read one of the

alcoholic's personal stories in the AA "Big Book" anyway. What happened was, I immediately identified, not with the details of the alcoholic's life but with the feelings described. Reading that, I suddenly had hope for the first time. If he felt like that and could stay sober, then so could I. I've been sober ever since.

—Michael, sober six years

My moment of realization came after reading Step 1 in the AA book *Twelve Steps and Twelve Traditions*. I'd read it before, often, but on this reading I suddenly accepted that I had the disease of addiction.

—Carole, sober three months

After reading a book called *The Christian Family*, I called on the Lord for help to stop my 17-year bulimia addiction—and the bulimia has never returned.

—Eleanor, 42, eating normally for 10 years

THAT TV TOUCH

It isn't just written words that can trigger moment-of-clarity experiences. Sometimes spoken words can jump out at us from TV screens:

Someone prayed for nicotine addicts on Christian TV, and I reacted by having an instant desire to stop smoking, which I did.

—Michelle, 57, cigarette-free eight years

It was the strangest thing. I touched a speaker on the TV screen and then called the number they flashed on the screen, and an hour later a woman arrived from AA and stayed two hours. It was then I knew I was free.

—Darlene, age 65, sober 12 years

I was watching this TV show about smoking, and from the information they gave, it was apparent to me that *I* was the type of smoker who had to go cold turkey, not taper off. So I quit cold turkey. That was 20 years ago.

—Bonnie, 57

DENIAL BUSTERS

When we collect evidence and facts—lots of facts—on a given subject, all in one convenient place, it becomes harder and harder not to see the truth. The same thing is true when we collect evidence and facts about our addiction. It becomes harder and harder to deny it. In the face of overwhelming evidence, an individual's denial is more likely to break down, which can trigger a moment-of-clarity healing. That's what happened to former First Lady Betty Ford. With professional help, the whole family met with her (the technique is called intervention) and confronted her with lots of facts about her addiction, her behaviors, and how all of it affected the rest of them. Faced with that, she capitulated and agreed to enter a chemical-dependency unit, where she apparently had her moment-of-clarity recovery.

You can do the same thing for yourself with facts. Right now you may be convinced that you don't have an addiction problem, or that your use of a substance or a behavior "isn't a problem." But if you're beginning to suspect that maybe your drinking, using, eating is "different" from most people's, then find out. Get the facts. Research it. Really go after those facts. Just taking the Johns Hopkins University Hospital 20-Question Test for Alcoholism made a big difference to me. I realize now it helped break down my denial before I went to my first self-help group meeting—so that when I got there, I was less defensive and more open for my jolt cure. So even if a fact isn't *the* silver dollar, it can be one of the silver dollars you need for your jackpot.

It takes a special kind of person to do this. Aside from answering that 20-question test (which was only hours before I turned myself in to the self-help group), I'm not one of them. I'm too good at denial. Get away from me with those facts! I don't want to know.

But maybe you're one of those people who can handle facts matter-of-factly, who will read an article one day and say, "I'm an alcoholic. I think I'll go to AA." There are people like this.

A friend of mine who has been sober in AA for 22 years handled all her addictions in one fell swoop: She quit drinking, smoking, pills, overeating, caffeine, and sugar—all in one day! One trigger fits all.

Of course, if it was merely a question of getting the *right* fact in front of an alcoholic, then we could print DRINKING IS BAD FOR YOU on a billboard over the freeway and cure thousands of commuters as they drove home from work. Obviously something else is involved.

While reading about an addiction can be a cure for some, for others it's just a way to escape the truth. Understanding one's addiction isn't the same as being free of it. My own stepfather read books on alcoholism and kept right on drinking until it killed him. We all know people like that. These are the intellectualizers. They are *not* the people who should bury themselves in libraries. They need something a little more earthy—like AA.

So if you're overwhelmed with reading material and you're still drinking, smoking, sniffing, overeating, or whatever, then let me share with you something *I* read this morning. It was the Thought for the Day that popped up on the screen when I turned on my computer: "If at first you don't succeed, try something else."

CHAPTER 9

Quiet Ways

If you are still, *it* speaks;
If you speak, *it* is still.

—Chinese expression

TAMING THE ADDICTED BRAIN

The Chinese say it politely. The anonymous groups put it a little more bluntly: "Sit down, shut up, and listen!" they'll tell a newcomer who starts to mouth-off.

There's a reason for this. Addicted people are notorious for talking too much, thinking too much, controlling too much, and trying to figure-it-all-out too much. They don't listen well, not to what's going on around them or to what's going on within. Most of them have no idea of what they really feel about things or what their real values are. That's all been put on hold while they focused on their addiction.

For many of the addicted, then, the Quiet Ways method of romancing a jolt cure, which means learning how to look inward using techniques such as meditation, is difficult. The very idea of looking inside for the truth is scary, like turning over a rock and finding creepy-crawly things. Plus sitting still for 20 minutes without eating, thinking, reading, talking, mulling, plotting, planning, worrying, projecting, smoking, or drinking, is unthinkable.

However, if you're one of those courageous ones who are strong enough to face what one alcoholic called "the gorilla within," then picking one of the Quiet Ways is probably one of the best things you can do to trigger a jolt cure—in which case you'll need to know more about what's involved.

SHHHH . . .

There are any number of ways to quiet down the mind and let the intuition show through. There are the formal ways, such as biofeedback and meditation, and there are the informal ways, such as gazing into a fire, driving a car (this is also one of the physical approaches to recovery), or sitting in a hot tub. History tells us that when Archimedes solved his hydraulic problem, he'd been taking a hot bath.

In the following case, a long-distance drive so quieted a man's mind that it brought on a jolt cure accidentally:

> I was driving down a road at night when suddenly the little man inside my gut said, "You're a real alcoholic, aren't you?" And at that moment I *knew* it was so. If that thought had gone through my conscious mind, I'd have defended against it. But this awareness came from my gut, so I was able to accept it.
>
> —*Walter, sober two years*

Self-hypnosis, silent chanting, float tanks, hypnosis, contemplation, guided imagery with tapes, rhythmic breathing, and focusing are all additional ways of lulling the mind so the mind chatter lets up long enough for some of our inner wisdom to show through. And when it does, a jolt cure can be the result.

MEDITATION

Probably one of the most popular of the Quiet Ways for romancing a jolt cure is meditation, which in Eastern cultures has been the preferred method of attaining healings and spiritual enlightenment for thousands of years. Here in the West we're just beginning to get comfortable with it.

> In a meditation, I had a vision of myself standing on a mountain-top, arms upstretched to God, saying, "Okay, I'm ready." I haven't had a drink or used drugs since that moment.
>
> —*Jessica, 34, sober one year*

There are plenty of good books on what meditation is and how to do it. You can take classes and go to workshops, but basically what they'll all tell you is that meditation is just sitting quietly and letting the truth (as opposed to the usual, gossipy mind chatter) reveal itself. "Truth" is that basic wisdom we all have hidden inside. Truth is what *is*, not necessarily what we need or want.

If you want to, you can start meditating right this minute—without taking a single class or reading a single book. Just close your eyes for about one minute (you can even do it at your desk—who will know?) and notice how busy your head is. That's your first and probably most valuable lesson about the mind and about meditating. Once you notice how busy the brain is, then you'll be ready for the next step, which is getting that mind to quiet down. *Not* easy to do. It's like trying *not* to think of peanuts. Some people do it by distracting themselves from their thinking by repeating a word they call a mantra. A nonsense syllable like *Da* will do just fine. Make one up. Some meditators like *Om*. If you're in a place in which you can leave your eyes closed for a few more minutes you can try repeating *Da* or *Om* to see if it helps unclutter your head. It probably won't. Your head will still be busy. Let it be. If you want, just for the fun of it, notice how many things you think about, how your thoughts flit from this to that. Remind you of a chicken?

When you meditate, it doesn't matter where you are, what time of day it is, what you wear, or where you put your hands. Sometimes I hold my hands in my lap, palms up and let the fingers touch each other. If after a few minutes I can't feel my fingers against each other, then I figure I must be in a meditative state. I don't know if that's true or not, but since it pleases me I don't really care. Another clue to being in a meditative state is if you jump a mile when the phone rings. Better unplug it if you can. If you want to "meditate" for as long as 20 minutes, go ahead. I find the first ten minutes are the hard part, chasing my busy mental "chicken" around, but after that I finally get into it—and then I hate to leave. You can trust your internal clock to keep time, use a kitchen timer, or open your eyes and peek at a real clock. It's not cheating. The only thing I'd recommend you *don't* do is meditate lying down. Too easy to fall asleep.

If you are still practicing your addiction, and the idea of meditation attracts you, you may end up like Freda:

> I had this experience of consciously going deeper into my soul than I had ever risked doing before, so much so that I was afraid of falling out the bottom into an abyss. Instead, I found this deep and unshakable sense of being whole, and I haven't had the obsession to drink since.
>
> —*Freda, 54, sober four years*

PRAYER

Probably the closest thing to meditation here in the West is prayer. If the idea of meditation strikes you as a little "fringe," you can do basically the same thing and call it praying. But too often prayer turns out to be more talking and petitioning for favors than listening for that "still small voice within" that tells us the truth about our situation. A minister I know, Reverend Clif King, wrote a book called *Two-Way Prayer* just to make this point: Prayer should be both talking *and* listening.

In his writing Emmet Fox describes prayer as we are discussing jolt cures here: "Prayer is the only thing that changes one's character." While a particular prayer session may bring only slight, incremental change, if you keep doing it, one day you'll suddenly get a "very strong realization of the presence of God" (his way of describing a moment-of-clarity experience), which will make a great and dramatic change in your character, "so that in the twinkling of an eye, your outlook, your habits, your whole life" will "completely change in every respect—which Jesus called being 'born again.' "

Many addicted people credit prayer as the thing that triggered their sudden healing moments.

> I'd suffered with bulimia for years. One night I was about to go into the kitchen and begin bingeing, after which I was going to go and vomit it up, but instead I got down on my knees and prayed for God to help me. When I got back up, I was calm. Instead of going into the kitchen I got into bed and slept right through the night with a full stomach from dinner, which is something I would never, ever have done! The next morning I ate a normal breakfast, and later I went to the market and shopped normally.
>
> —*Beryl, 20, eating normally for five years*

> I woke up at 3 A.M., looked at the moon, and said, God, please help me. The next day I checked into a detox center for my alcoholism.
>
> —*Dulcie, 58, sober one year*

CONTEMPLATION

In a less formal way than either meditation or prayer, simple contemplation—staring into space or otherwise resting the brain—can sometimes trigger jolt cures. The most common way of resting the brain, of course, is sleep:

To Sleep . . .

Sleeping is a Quiet Way of getting past the busy mind chatter and into the intuitive mind. Many addicted people have their moment-of-clarity experiences upon awakening—before their defenses have had time to arise also:

> I woke up one morning and realized I couldn't go on anymore the way I was going. Suddenly I was willing to do whatever it would take to get sober. And that's what I did.
>
> —*Dale G., 26, sober one year*

> I'd gone through a treatment program, but I didn't think I was an alcoholic, so it didn't work. But four months later I awoke from a

three-day blackout and had a moment of clarity in which I knew that if I didn't get to AA I would be dead. I've been sober ever since.

—*Nicole, 24, sober two years*

I had been fat all my life. On February 8, 1987, I awakened with a start. It suddenly dawned on me that if I didn't do something about my weight, I would die. The next day I bought an exercise bike and put myself on 1800 calories a day. On November 9, 1987, I reached my target weight. On February 8, 1988, I celebrated my first anniversary of maintenance.

—*signed Slim, Happy, and Healthy, Ann Landers,*
Los Angeles Times, *January 16, 1989*

. . . *Perchance to Dream*

Here's a case in which a woman's dreams seemed to be doing more for her than she was doing for herself:

I was dating a doctor who supplied me with the very best drugs. I had no reason to quit. But in a dream I saw myself at an AA meeting on the floor in front of a podium, as before an altar. Not long after that somebody took me to an AA meeting and it looked exactly like my dream and that was my moment of clarity. I knew then that I was on my way to life.

—*Hillary, 20s, sober seven months*

Mirror, Mirror on the Wall

I think it's interesting that for many people the moment of truth is triggered by gazing out a window or looking into a mirror. They literally "see" themselves as they truly are. Perhaps what happens here is that the busy brain, which is so full of denial, takes some time out. During this brief rest period, some of the defenses drop for a moment, and the truth skates through. I can remember such a moment myself about two years before I finally stopped drinking. One morning, hung over again, I gazed out my bedroom window and "realized," as though for the first time, that my life was crumbling. It wasn't *the* moment for me. I kept on drinking. But it was a critical part of the buildup to my jolt cure, which happened later on.

In my files I have the case of a young woman who had two major life-changing moments (in the area of personal relationships, not addiction) in this manner. One happened at 18 when she was looking into a mirror combing her hair. The other happened at age 26 when she was looking out the window.

Here are some "mirror" cases in the addiction area:

One night I was looking at myself in my bathroom mirror. Suddenly instead of my face I saw this skid-row scene. I saw myself sitting on a curb like a bum. I knew that would be me if I kept up my cocaine use. It changed my whole outlook; and I've had a totally different attitude ever since.

—*Mitch, 32, sober six months*

I was at work. I went to the liquor store at lunch and bought a pint and ran back to work. I went into the bathroom and opened it and began to drink it. At that moment I caught a look at myself in the mirror, drinking this pint in the bathroom, and I saw what I'd become.

—*Barb, 45, sober six years*

Sometimes resting the brain by gazing out a window, in much the same way as gazing into a fire or staring at a candle in meditation, can allow new material to spring forth into awareness:

I was drinking myself more and more into an example of a typical, isolated, woman "closet" drinker. One day I looked through the shutters of my windows, and they looked like prison bars. I thought, "Is this the way my life is going to be from now on?" I began to cry, and then I called my doctor. Two days later I was in a treatment center.

—*Sharon, 56, sober six years*

I'd slipped. I was discouraged. I was just standing there at the sink washing dishes, looking out the window, feeling bad, when suddenly everything I saw looked really bright. Suddenly I had hope. I knew I'd try again, and this time I'd be okay.

—Jodie, 18, sober 11 months

I'd had a bad slip. In a matter of a week my cocaine problem had increased tenfold. One day I was in this store, looking out the window at the street. I was watching this old bum, ambling along—and then I looked out to the street and saw this guy driving along in a nice car. Suddenly I saw—and I really *felt* it—that I had a choice. I could go the way of the bum, or the way of the guy in the car. I knew if I kept on using, I'd end up like that bum in no time flat. Right then and there I decided to stop. Today I feel entirely different inside. This time I just know it's going to be okay.

—Victor, 30s, back in hospital and sober three weeks

FACING THE TRUTH

On my second day in the treatment center I said to myself, "I'm going to make these 21 days work!" I decided I'd start by not telling any more lies. My father flew out from Chicago, and I told him I was a cocaine addict, which I'd always projected would kill him. But it didn't kill him. Truth doesn't kill, it heals.

—Saul, 30s, sober two years

For addicted people, the ultimate goal of mind-quieting techniques such as meditation and prayer is to face the truth, including the truth about one's own addiction.

The truth does indeed set you free. But it can't be "figured out." Truth just washes over you in meditation or when you're in prayer and you "know" it. Once seen, it seems obvious. You wonder how you could have been so blind as to miss it.

I had a silent but clear insight that the way I'd always seen myself was a *lie*. At that very moment I became different.

—Cherie, 39, has maintained weight loss for five years

One night a simple truth occurred to me: I was never going to win. I haven't gambled since.

—Lawrence, has abstained from gambling for 18 months

And for TJ, the moment of truth cured two addictions at once:

> I'd just lost $8,500 at the track and had a $350 bar bill. I stood there and said to myself, "I don't have $2 in my pocket, and there's no gas in my car. I will never gamble or drink again." And I haven't.
>
> *—TJ, 50s, sober and a non-gambler 20 years*

> I'd been smoking two packs a day since I was 11 years old. One day, at age 23, I stared at the lit end of my cigarette and realized I'd been inhaling this fire and smoke into my lungs. I asked myself, "Why do you want to inhale this stuff into your lungs?" And I stopped, just like that.
>
> *—Jessie, cigarette-free four years*

Don't assume you'll be one of the people who takes a long time to have a moment-of-clarity healing. It has nothing to do with the severity of your illness or your past performance. I assumed it would take me a long time (three to five years) to stop drinking once I went to that community self-help group meeting, and I was wrong. It happened the first night.

So each time you go, put in your silver dollars and you just hope like crazy that *this* time the slot machine delivers.

Chapter *10*

Brain Ways

—*Lance Wolstrup, computer programmer*

What if you've already tried the other suggested ways of romancing a jolt cure and none of them clicked for you? What if you've gone to meetings-meetings-meetings, you've jogged and meditated, you've read until your eyes are blurry, and you're *still* drinking or eating yourself silly? You know it's time to try something else, but what?

It's at this stage of the game you probably wish you could hook yourself up to your computer and zap yourself sober with a computer program such as the one above.

The program isn't real, of course, it's a joke—at least for now. But maybe someday it will be possible to attach an electrode to our brain, input a tidy little "addiction recovery" subroutine, and with a single keystroke create an instant jolt cure.

The trouble with any kind of computer/brain analogy is this: As we saw in Chapter 4 in the discussion of the biochemistry of the brain, the fact that each of the brain's 10 to 100 billion neurons is connected to thousands of others means that the brain can work on a number of things simultaneously, whereas the computer, albeit fast, can only do one task at a time.

According to the *Newsweek* article on the brain mentioned in that chapter, "Computers think too straight. Computers don't do the kind of thinking where there is an almost instantaneous flash of recognition—the kind you or I get when figuring out a problem."

Nor, it seems, do computers do the kind of thinking that brings on a moment-of-clarity healing. What does that is the brain.

THE ADDICT'S FAVORITE QUESTION

One question recovering addicts and alcoholics love to ask each other is: If they came out with a pill that cured addiction so you could drink or use other drugs normally, would you take it? Surprisingly, the answer to this is almost always no. First, because most of us who have "been there" can't imagine drinking or using normally. The addict's philosophy, after all, is: anything worth doing is worth *over*doing—so what would be the point? Better not to do it at all.

The second reason for the no is because most of us have become hooked on sobriety. We've discovered that the natural highs our brain chemistry gives us are enough. Not only do we have an inner physician, but, according to Norman Cousins, we have an inner pharmacy. We have thousands of brain secretions that, in their proper combinations, can provide "cures" for most of what ails us, but because most of us got addicted to outside things early in life, we never had a chance to find that out.

THE MYSTERIOUS BRAIN

The brain, despite all we're learning about it, is still an overwhelming mystery. We'd probably have to build a computer a mile high and the size of Texas to duplicate all its calculations, maneuvers, and functions. There's so much we don't know—including how instant healing occurs.

Those Hidden Variables

But just because we can't look into the brain and see the cause of instant healing doesn't mean it's not there—or somewhere. Many thinkers, including Einstein, have been uncomfortable with the idea put forth by quantum mechanics that there are such things as causeless or nonlinear events in nature—which is what a jolt cure appears to be. They insist that the explanation for such events is lurking behind the scenes in "hidden variables." Other thinkers, however, assert that spontaneous, non-causal (or non-*caused*) leaps to health *do* take place. This debate promises to heat up in the years to come.

One good analogy for the "hidden variable" side is the cassette-tape player vs. the record player. If you fast-forward a cassette tape from song number one to song number three, you can actually hear the intervening "steps" whizzing by. But with a record, if you want to go from song one to three, you have to *lift* the needle off the record before putting it back down again. From the record's point of view, this may *seem* like a causeless, nonlinear leap, but that's because the record doesn't know about the existence of your arm—the hidden variable behind the "miraculous" leap. Jolt cures may be the same. There may well be some hidden variable in the brain that we don't know about. From our point of view it seems as though "God just picked me up and flew me over to the other side, and I was healed."

No "Seat of Addiction"

We've certainly *looked* for these hidden variables, that's for sure. Since the days of phrenology, a school of psychology that hoped to find explanations for human behavior by studying the bumps on the head, science has investigated every nook and cranny of the brain and, so far at least, no "seat of addiction" and no "cause of instant healing" has been found.

NONDRUG WAYS TO ALTER BRAIN CHEMISTRY

Ultimately everything we do affects the brain, even reading the morning paper. But some methods are more direct than others. As far as brain chemistry is concerned, getting "high" on heroin or speed is obviously faster and more direct than getting "high" on looking at a beautiful sunset.

The drug companies, now aided by computers, are zeroing in on developing a pill for every ill. Someday we may indeed have a pill to cure chronic depression (scientists are close to that now), autism, psychosis, schizophrenia, obsession, and of course, addiction. But in a book about addiction it doesn't seem kosher to be even thinking about trying to romance a jolt cure by ingesting chemicals! Maybe it's lucky such pills don't exist yet and we're not faced with these ethical choices.

Our purpose here is to find recovery without having to resort to chemicals, especially mind-altering chemicals that, with very few exceptions, are off-limits to recovering addicts and alcoholics.

Our task is to find some ways, less direct than drugs and pills but good ways nonetheless, to impact our brain chemistry and trigger a jolt cure.

For Starters—Stop!

Obviously one of the biggest changes you can make in your brain chemistry is to *stop* drinking, drugging, smoking, over-eating, and obsessing over people and substances because it keeps our chemistry in an uproar. One alcoholic blackout can kill lots of brain cells. (Since I was a blackout drinker, I've killed off my share, I'm sure. Maybe if I hadn't done that I'd have finished this book a lot sooner.)

The addicted brain is all out of whack, and we need to get it back on track again. Good living will do wonders. But of course, that's your dilemma! You *know* that, but in order to stop your addiction you need a moment of clarity to show you the way.

These are some general nondrug ways of changing your brain chemistry and, hopefully, your mind: acupuncture, biofeedback, fasting, foods, herbs (not hallucinogenic!), vitamins, and even water.

Since I am not an expert in any one of these areas, I'm reluctant to expound on them at greater length than I do here. What I do know is that the material available on these subjects is considerable. Should you want it, it's there.

Here are a few books you can start off with and take it from there. Most of them have good book lists in the back if you want additional suggestions:

The Nutrition Detective, Nan Kathryn Fuchs, Ph.D. (Tarcher); *Life Extension,* Durk Pearson and Sandy Shaw (Warner Books); *The Pritikin Promise,* Nathan Pritikin (Pocket Books); *Minding the Body, Mending the Mind,* Joan Borysenko, Ph.D. (Addison-Wesley); *Mind as Healer, Mind as Slayer,* Kenneth R. Pelletier (Delta); *Psychoneuroimmunology,* Robert Ader, ed.; Norman Cousins, *Anatomy of an Illness* (Norton); Bernie S. Siegel, *Love, Medicine & Miracles* (Harper & Row).

Suffice it to say that they all have an impact on our chemistry. When we're talking about things we eat and otherwise ingest, such as food and vitamins, it's obvious. It's perhaps less obvious when we're talking about something such as acupuncture.

Acupuncture

This technique for treating pain or disease originated in China thousands of years ago and consists of inserting hair-thin needles into the skin at specific points of the body and leaving them there for a period of time, maybe half an hour, maybe an hour. (There is also acupressure, which involves body massage or electronic stimulation but no puncturing of the skin.)

Occasionally, although this is not its stated medical purpose, acupuncture can trigger a jolt cure. Maybe this is because the procedure stirs up our endorphins, which are the opiatelike chemicals in our brain that make us feel good, and when that happens we see things differently (world-view shift)—and when we see things differently, a healing can be the result.

From my own experience, I can vouch for acupuncture as a natural way to alter your consciousness. I've had a series of treatments twice—once for back (disc) pain and once for a leg injury (from aerobics). Aside from helping me physically, it helped me psychologically. While lying on the acupuncture table looking like a porcupine with those needles sticking out of me, I had some insights that helped me end a relationship "addiction." So I know it's possible.

Biofeedback

Biofeedback is a technique, using special monitoring instruments hooked up to the body, of learning how to regulate body functions such as heartbeat, body temperature, and even brainwave pattern. (Meditators have been able to do these sorts of things to their bodies for centuries, but we Westerners didn't believe it until we could see results and get feedback from a machine.) Biofeedback has been a popular stress fighter in business and industry for years. And there are no needles involved.

I haven't yet had any personal experience with biofeedback other than seeing demonstrations, so I can't tell you what it feels like. You'll have to discover that on your own. One woman I saw monitored while she meditated got "feedback" by hearing a buzz. The deeper she went into her meditative state, the more pronounced was the buzz. That was her "proof" that she was indeed meditating.

Obviously, being able to do things to your body, such as lower your blood pressure, change your heart rate, and lower your anxiety level, has broad implications from the brain-chemistry point of view. You can't do things like this *without* changing your brain chemistry. And a chemical change in the brain one minute could be a jolt cure the next.

Food and Vitamins

If you want to "change your mind" by changing your chemistry, to me the most logical place to start is with food and vitamins. There's an overwhelming amount of material here, since nutrition, like addiction, is very "in" these days. By tonight you could come home with enough material to write a master's thesis. There are books, magazines, tapes, classes, and articles galore. Most health-food and vitamin stores have employees who'd be happy to help you get started. A lot of the information is contradictory, but if you're willing to work at it, maybe it's the way to go.

They say you are what you eat. If you don't like what you are, then maybe you ought to change what you eat. That seems simple enough.

Maybe you're eating the wrong things, and it's affecting your brain chemistry in a negative way. Maybe you're eating too much and that's your addiction. Or too little. Whatever it is you're doing, chances are it is affecting your brain.

There are certainly enough theories about specific foods: meat makes you angry; sugar makes you crazy; wheat makes you crave alcohol; milk makes you sleepy. In Weight Watchers and Overeaters Anonymous they talk about "red lights," which are foods (usually the ones we like) that trigger destructive eating binges. They should be avoided, just as the alcoholic has to avoid all alcohol for the same reason: It sets up a craving for more.

Vitamins and herbs can affect us, too. Some people say vitamins aren't necessary so long as we "eat the right things." My own experience is that I feel better if I take vitamins. So I take vitamins. I hate vitamins, but I take them. And if I eat well, too (which for me means fruits, vegetables, grains, lots of water, and no red meat), I feel a whole lot better.

In fact, I'm convinced that these things helped me stop my smoking addiction. This is what I did: I followed romance method number one. I put my body where they were talking about my primary problem (smoking groups). Twice I made the pre-jolt phase (meaning I stopped, but I was biting the bullet). I had two relapses, one after seven months, one after three weeks. The third time I had a moment of clarity (when it happened, I recognized it for what it was) and that put me into the post-jolt phase of recovery. I haven't smoked since. That was 14 years ago. The only reason I bring this up here is because I'm convinced that the fact that I was on a health kick just before I went to that last smoking group (I was eating well, jogging, and taking vitamins) had a lot to do with my eventual jolt cure. It paved the way.

So consider that what you order for dinner tonight could affect your gambling or cocaine addiction down the line.

JUST START SOMEWHERE

On the healing journey, it doesn't really matter where you begin; just start somewhere. Even if it's going to the wrong meeting, reading the wrong book, doing the wrong exercise, being in the wrong treatment center, talking to the wrong counselor, or eating the wrong thing. So what? Sooner or later you'll figure it out, and then you can correct your course. In the meantime, it gets your "healing juices" going—it gets you in gear.

Besides, where is it written that only the "right" treatment can trigger a jolt recovery?

CHAPTER *11*

Contrary Ways

Opposites are cures for opposites.
Hippocrates, c. 460–400 B.C., *Breaths,* Book I

In the commonwealth I would by contraries
Execute all things; for no kind of traffic
Would I admit; no name of magistrate;
Letters should not be known; riches, poverty
And use of service, none; contract, succession,
Bourn, bound of land, tilth, vineyard, none;
No use of metal, corn, or wine, or oil;
No occupation; all men idle, all;
And women too, but innocent and pure.
—*William Shakespeare,* The Tempest

FLY TO FRANCE

Sometimes in working with alcoholic or addicted patients I can almost feel it in my bones when they need to break loose and do something outlandish—something really *contrary.*

Frank is just such a case. Now in his mid-fifties, he has been drinking for 30 years. For 20 of those 30 years he's been trying to stop. Over and over, he'd go to treatment, relapse, and start again. "Nothing can surrender me," he often says, almost proudly. "The more they push, the more I resist." Frank is also a downer, dour and depressed, unable to have any fun at all.

81

There's just no life in him. Recently he checked back into our hospital after yet another slip. One day when I walked into the group room and saw him sitting there with the usual woe-is-me look on his face, I blurted out, "Frank, for Christ's sake, fly to France!" He looked at me as if I'd shot him. Then he got up and walked out.

So far, no France—and no sobriety. But somehow I think I got to him because he told his wife (a patient of mine) about the outlandish thing I'd said. "I hear you told Frank he should fly to France," she said to me a few weeks later, no doubt thinking *I* must be nuts. "He keeps talking about it," she went on. "He keeps bringing it up."

Mmmm, I thought. I think I put a bug in his ear.

"Remind him that he's got the money to do it," I said to her. "You will mention that, won't you?" She nodded. And who knows, maybe one day the wife will send me a postcard from Paris, saying Frank is sober at last and they're on a second honeymoon.

Contrariness, it seems, can play a role in some addiction recoveries. People get stuck in ruts, and some of them, like Frank, have a built-in aversion to surrender. In 20 years on the battleground of alcoholism, he has defeated everyone who's tried to help him sober up, including his first wife. This wife is new.

Still, somewhere inside Frank, and others like him, there lies a sober man screaming to get out, a Titanic just waiting for his iceberg, somebody who is probably tired of the fight and would like nothing better than to "surrender to win."

I don't think a moment-of-clarity experience will happen to Frank on his own turf. He's been too defensive too long for that. His best chance, I think, is to go away—someplace far away, someplace he's never been, a place he knows little about. Maybe in such a setting his defenses will let down just a bit. Just enough.

That he can afford it is encouraging. That he won't *do* it is frustrating. But that's Frank!

ON THE CONTRARY

Are you still fighting the good, stubborn fight? Is there something about Frank with which you identify? Just a little? If so, maybe one of the Contrary Ways is the romance method you should try for your addiction.

Samba Lessons

It may just be that picking something contrary to do, something unrelated to your addiction and unrelated to anything you've tried before, such as taking samba lessons, will trigger a jolt cure. Sound crazy? Maybe, but there are times when you have to go clear out of the ballpark to catch the ball.

Heart's Desire

Sometimes it's in the area of our "heart's desire" that we end up finding the Contrary Way that triggers our moment-of-clarity healing. Think about it. What's *your* heart's desire? What activities or adventures attract you (other than your addiction, of course)? What is it you'd like to do but don't have the time for? What would you consider to be totally impractical, but fun?

One of the best ways to get ideas for Contrary Ways is to look through catalogs for adult-education classes and see what hits you with a "Hey, I'd like to do that!" feeling. It does *not* have to be something related to your problem, your responsibilities, or your work. It's supposed to be something contrary, remember?

My very favorite catalog is the University of California, Los Angeles (UCLA), extension catalog, 250 pages of wonderfully contrary and escapist things to do. You can send for it no matter where you are and pore over it for ideas. There are courses, workshops, trips, seminars, weekends, and adventures. It's delicious. That's where I found that white-water river-raft trip I took. I've also taken Greek Dancing, Stained-Glass-Window Making, and Previewing New Movies—none of which have anything to do with my life, but they sounded like fun. Adult education is another popular field now, so your chance of getting the information you need is good. Check your local newspapers, high schools, colleges and universities (if there are any), and pick yourself a winning contrary cure.

PARADOXICAL WAYS

Sometimes addiction-recovery groups such as AA use the contrary approach intuitively. The AA old-timer, much like the Zen master, knows you can't always solve a problem at the level of the problem. A newcomer who comes to him complaining about a marriage or job crisis is likely to be told to drive some other newcomer to an AA meeting. "What the hell has *that* got to do with my problem?" the frustrated newcomer may ask.

The answer is nothing—and everything. Doing something contrary or unrelated to the problem at hand "works" because it's a way of resting the brain and letting the unconscious, sometimes the wiser part of the mind, go to work. If you have a crisis in area X, AA says, take care of business over in area Y and Z, and eventually the solution to the problem in area X will appear. It's a paradox.

Addiction recovery is full of paradoxes—statements that seem absurd and contrary, but may actually be true. A common one is, "The cure for alcoholism is drinking." Absurd, yes. And also true. If you drink and keep drinking, sooner or later you'll get so sick from it you'll want to stop. Hence, drinking cures alcoholism.

Aversion therapy is a paradox cure. Patients smoke, drink, or eat until they get physically sick and (we hope) don't want to do it anymore.

When the paradoxical approach to addiction healing is carried to an extreme, it's called "hitting bottom." Sometimes hitting bottom just means that things get worse. But sometimes it results in a jolt healing.

We'll look at Hitting Bottom next.

Change occurs when we become what we are, not when we try to become what we are not.

—*Arnold Breisser, Ph.D.,*
The Paradoxical Theory of Change

CHAPTER *12*

Hitting Bottom

The most significant transitions involve a time in hell.
—*William Bridges in* Transitions: Making Sense of
Life's Changes

Spiritual enlightenment occurs only when a person
has been through dark and disturbing trials of the
soul.
—*John Sanford,* Healing and Wholeness

THE WRISTWATCH TEST

In the early days of Alcoholics Anonymous it was said that if
you still owned a wristwatch, you hadn't yet "hit bottom."

What does hitting bottom mean? It means you have reached
a point in your addiction where it all seems utterly futile,
where there's nothing but discouragement and failure, where it
appears that the only solution is to give up and say, "This is the
end!"

It is at just such a time that a moment-of-clarity healing can
happen. The suffering itself triggers the jolt cure. It has happened this way to many.

High Bottom, Low Bottom

Originally, hitting bottom was seen in terms of material
losses—loss of one's job, home, car, status, and finally, wrist-

watch. But that was because people waited until they'd lost all these things before they sought treatment. But as AA grew and more treatments for all addictions became easily available, it became clear that there are bottoms—and then there are bottoms. There are "low bottom" drunks (meaning those who *have* lost everything), and there are "high bottom" or "silk sheet" drunks (meaning those who haven't). There are also different ways of bottoming out—physical, psychological, and spiritual ways as well as material ways.

No Rules Anymore

The more experience we have, it seems, the less we know about recovery. Something simple like the wristwatch test doesn't work anymore, if it ever did. Today there are just no rules about bottoming out. Each of us comes to the end of our rope in our own unique way and in our own time. For an overeater, hitting bottom might mean being 20 pounds overweight—or 200 pounds overweight. One of my own bottoms for my smoking addiction was my coughing. I hated the coughing. Eventually it was that that paved the way for my jolt cure.

As long as we think something will keep us from hitting bottom (in other words, will keep us from pain), that's probably what we'll try. That's normal. Pain is no fun at all. But in the end, if the other methods we've tried in our attempts to romance a jolt recovery don't work, we may discover that the bottom is staring us right in the face.

An ashtray is what made this man hit his smoking bottom:

> I woke up one morning, looked at my dirty ashtray, and said, "Yuck!" I haven't had a cigarette since.
> —*Man calling in to a radio talk show on addiction recovery*

In this next case, hitting bottom meant death. This woman drank again after her moment of clarity and treatment and died at only 28:

I came into the hospital after I had a terrifying dream that I drank a whole bottle of vodka, and died. In the dream my sister was shaking me. I woke up in a cold sweat and said "That's it. I'm getting help."

—*Kathy, 28*

CONSEQUENCES

A few years ago a TV news reporter asked a small-town mayor what, in his opinion, was the cure for crime. The mayor didn't wait a beat before answering. "Punishment," he shot back.

Sometimes punishment, in the form of the painful consequences arising from addictive behaviors, is the only thing that gets an alcoholic's or addict's attention. Job loss, divorce, arrest, jail, financial ruin, physical illness, accident, humiliation, embarrassment. Any one of these could trigger a jolt cure. When it doesn't, additional consequences follow.

When they put handcuffs on me and pushed me into the squad car and talked to me like I was a slut and a criminal, I was humiliated. I had a moment of clarity right then and there. That was not only my last drunken-driving arrest, it was my last drunk—period.

—*Evelyn, 40s, sober 10 years*

Comedian Richard Pryor apparently hit bottom and had a jolt cure when he set himself on fire while freebasing cocaine. He nearly died:

If anybody was born again, I was. In the hospital I said, "I want to live. I'm going to get out of here!" Now I see people doing drugs, and I get sad. Those gaps you fill with drugs aren't helping.

—*Pryor, in* People *magazine*

This man had an automobile accident, which was painful enough, and then there was some humiliation thrown in:

I was drunk and had an auto accident in the rain. I was hurt. I walked to a house and knocked, but the couple who opened it couldn't even understand me because I was babbling and I scared them. They gave me a look I'll never forget—I was slime. They slammed the door in my face. Then the truth struck me like a tap on the back of the head: You don't *have* to live like this anymore. I walked into town and checked into a hospital. From there I went to a treatment center, and I've been sober ever since.

—Peter, 26, sober two years

For the addicted individual, each and every episode of pain is just another silver dollar in the slot machine that brings it closer to the jackpot (or jolt recovery) we're hoping for. It's a kind of do-it-yourself aversion therapy. We overdo our addiction to the point where it makes us sick.

The Fear Trigger

Here, it's a painful emotion, fear, that triggers a jolt cure:

A friend of mine was in the hospital with open-heart surgery. The doctor came out and said, "If he hadn't smoked, he wouldn't have had to have heart surgery." At that moment I said to myself, "I'll never smoke another cigarette!" That was eight years ago, and I've never even had the desire or want for a cigarette.

—James, 30s, cigarette-free eight years

The Anger Trigger

Another painful emotion, anger, triggers this moment of clarity:

When my psychiatrist in the treatment center told me she didn't think I'd stay sober unless I went to live in a halfway house after my discharge, I was absolutely furious. My first reaction was, "How dare she! I'll show her. I'll stay sober out of spite just to prove to her she's wrong!" I never went to the halfway house, and I've been sober ever since.

—Jan, 55, sober seven years

PAIN KEEPS PUSHING

Nobody *has* to change, but if you decide you want to, then you're the one who's got to do the work. The responsibility for change always belongs to the one who's in pain. If the other six methods for romancing an instant change didn't do anything for you, then it looks as though Hitting Bottom might put you far enough out on a limb for you to say, "I've had it."

> When it begins to feel like death; when you think it's a catastrophe; when it's the end of everything and it's all slipping away—that's when recovery happens.
> —*Father T., 40s, sober 15 years*

Keep on Keeping On

What you do first is keep right on doing what you've been doing all along. You keep on drinking, drugging, gambling, eating, smoking, shopping. The only difference is, as I said earlier, this time do it consciously. Notice what you're up to, how it's affecting your day-to-day life and, if you can, how you feel about it. What emotions are going on?

Obviously this isn't something a person still in denial is going to do, but, surprisingly, there are some who will do it, who are already doing it. For example, at a Weight Watchers meeting, where writing down what you eat is part of the program, a woman told the group that even though she wasn't yet ready to stop stuffing herself, she was at least writing down what she stuffed herself with: "Even if it's 32 cookies, two pints of chocolate chocolate-chip ice cream and one medium jar of chunky peanut butter, it all goes down on this sheet of paper!"

The Pain Diary

Try this for one month. Buy a little pocket-size spiral notebook. On each new page for about 30 pages, put down the following, leaving a line between each entry:

Today's Date:
Work:
Family/Friends:
Health:
Legal:
Financial:
Emotional:

Then once a day for a month fill in how each of these major life areas was affected by your problem or, if you're not afraid of the word, by your addiction. A drinker's notebook entry for one day might look like this:

Work: Half hour late today.
Family/Friends: Girlfriend pissed off. Argument. She's nagging me more about drinking.
Health: Hangover.
Legal: Lawyer called re: DUI case coming up.
Financial: Spent $45 (maybe more) on drinks.
Emotional: Anxious. Shaky. Don't like reading this stuff at all!

Each awareness, each truth one faces, is a silver dollar. They *can* add up and turn into a jackpot.

You don't have to let anybody know you're writing these things down. They're for your eyes only. Do it secretly if you have to, but do it. There's something magical about getting things out of your head and down on paper. It focuses your attention on your problem. When you see something written down, it's much harder to deny it.

Here's a smoker's entry:

Work: Was thinking of quitting job because of new no-smoking rules.
Family/Friends: Kids bugging me again about smoking. Brought home literature from school.
Health: Coughing as usual. Woke up with stabbing pain at the base of my sternum.
Legal: No problem here that I know of.
Financial: Bought another carton.
Emotional: Nervous. Irritable.

An overweight patient of mine noticed that some of her entries were the same day after day, along with some new information:

Work: Still avoiding job hunting because of how I look.
Family/Friends: Turned down blind date and family reunion. Too embarrassed by how I look.
Health: Aware that carrying around this weight isn't good for my heart.
Legal: Cop gave me ticket for weaving. I'd been trying to open a bag of chips!
Financial: Sticking with low-paying job because I'm avoiding job hunting.
Emotional: Feel stuck. Feel like black sheep. Angry.

Eventually, if you can force yourself to do this—and yes, it's hard!—you'll have to face some truths. It may be the realization (that could come as an aha!) that the prices you're paying to maintain your addiction far outweigh the benefits. The aha! might just be your jolt cure.

Have a Hangover

In addition to noticing the consequences of your problem or addiction, make an attempt *not* to minimize these consequences. What I mean by this is, if you have a hangover, have a hangover. Don't numb it with aspirin or soothe your stomach with Alka-Seltzer. And no "hair of the dog"! Don't "enable" yourself. Pay the full price. Let yourself be sick and miserable as Mother Nature meant you to be. You deserve it! Hopefully it'll bring you to your knees just a little bit faster and trigger your life-saving jolt cure.

The alternative is most unpleasant. Here's the case of a woman who finally realized this:

I was in my bedroom with my TV, my remote control, my telephone, and my case of wine. Suddenly it dawned on me that this is what *hell* must be like! They put you in a room with all the booze you can ever drink, a TV, and a phone, and you can never leave the room. You have to stay there and get worse and worse. *That's* when I got help. I went and got treatment and haven't had a drink since. I just didn't want to live in hell!

—*Frances, age 29, sober three years*

That's the purpose of the Hitting Bottom method of romancing a jolt cure—to show you hell ahead of time so you don't have to end up living there.

PART 3

AFTER
THE
JOLT RECOVERY

CHAPTER 13

Maintaining Your Jolt Recovery

A young Boston policeman went up to the door of a house in which a crazy man had barricaded himself. When the policeman demanded that the man come out, the man blasted the policeman right through the wooden door and killed him. Later a reporter went down to the police station. "How could that happen?" the reporter asked. "I thought that was the most basic part of a policeman's training—never to stand in front of a door when someone inside may have a gun." "That's simple," the police captain said. "He forgot."

—*story told by Verne W. at an AA meeting*

DON'T FORGET

For recovering alcoholics and addicts, the moral of this story is obvious: Don't forget.

Don't forget who you are, where you are, and what you're doing there. Don't forget that you can't drink and you can't use mind-altering chemicals (or whatever)—*no matter what*. If your attention gets diverted from this, it could put you in danger of relapse. This is one of the main reasons recovering people still refer to themselves as "alcoholic," "addict," "compulsive overeater," or "compulsive gambler" even if they've been abstinent for years. It's so they don't forget.

"For the alcoholic," warns the "big book," *Alcoholics Anonymous*, what's important is "the maintenance and growth of a spiritual experience"—in other words, the jolt cure.

Looking for Bricks

In the story of *The Three Little Pigs*, the pigs knew that getting that house made of bricks would make them safe from the big, bad wolf. No matter how hard he huffed and he puffed, he just couldn't blow that brick thing down.

Unfortunately, sobriety doesn't have the same guarantees. Looking for bricks is useless. There's no safe-house anywhere, including length of sobriety. You'll notice that after each quote throughout this book I put the speaker's name and the length of his or her sobriety or abstinence. But that can change in a minute—even for the people with lots of years under their belts. Statistically, some of the sober people in this book, by the time it's published, will be drunk. As Linus said in the "Peanuts" cartoon, "There's no safety in numbers—or anything else." The number of years of sobriety that people have doesn't make them invulnerable, immune to relapse. It's not an inoculation. If they take a drink, it means absolutely nothing. It all goes right back to zero days of sobriety.

As AA says, "We are all just one drink away from a drunk." The purpose of this chapter is to give you some ways to keep that from happening.

Maintaining a jolt cure takes work. Fortunately, there is no raging obsession to deal with, so you should be feeling fairly comfortable as you proceed on the maintenance road.

Give Yourself the Quick Post-Jolt Test

Sometimes people wishfully *think* they've been jolted sober, but it's not true. Even though they really want it and have the best of intentions, sooner or later the lack of commitment that goes hand in hand with the pre-jolt phase surfaces, they find the maintenance work too much trouble, and they relapse.

One way to help you determine which phase you're in is to answer this question honestly: If right this minute, feeling as you do now, you found yourself alone in a room in a distant city with your "drug of choice," would you use it? People in the post-jolt phase usually say no immediately. People in the pre-jolt phase seem ambivalent: "Well, gosh, that's hard. I don't know. That depends on the circumstances. I might. I'd certainly *try* not to . . ." A "no, but—" answer is almost always a yes.

What was your answer?

Hard Versus Easy

The common assumption about lifelong abstinence is that it's "hard," that the recovering addict, alcoholic, smoker, gambler, or overeater has to struggle constantly with an overwhelming temptation 24 hours a day, seven days a week.

Fortunately, this is not true. This description fits what many pre-jolt people experience, but not what most of the post-jolt people feel. The truth is, for many recovering people who have had jolt cures, abstinence is unexpectedly easy. Here's a woman who experienced both phases. The difference is obvious:

> I drank daily for 22 years. I couldn't *not* drink even for one day. Then I went to AA and bit the bullet for three months. It was awful. Fortunately, before I dropped out and drank again, I had this moment of clarity, and since then I haven't even had an urge to drink. It's been a snap.
>
> —*Roberta, 40s, sober four years*

This qualitative difference is what makes the moment-of-clarity cure so desirable. Few of us could handle the pre-jolt phase for more than a few weeks or months. If I'd had to stay there I'd have jumped ship long ago. That's no way to live. AA calls it "white-knuckle sobriety." Some people may last as long as a year, but they're usually not much fun to be with in the meantime. They complain constantly about how hard sobriety is, how much pain they're in, how it's not worth it—and sometimes you find yourself wishing they *would* drink. Sooner or later they probably will. Either that, or they'll have a jolt cure.

FLATTEN OUT YOUR DRAMA CURVE

One change in your life that will begin to happen automatically (and you should definitely help it along) is a gradual flattening out of your "drama curve."

If you're like most addicted people, you are probably used to lots of drama, chaos, and crisis in your life—usually an outward manifestation of what's going on inside. In general, people who are settled on the inside don't have drama on the outside. I've gotten so that I avoid crisis-prone people like the plague. With them, everything is a big deal. They have no time for creativity. They have no time to get to know themselves. They are much too busy putting out fires. It's exhausting to them and everybody around them.

Drugs and alcohol, as well as food and frantic crisis behaviors, are "numb-ers." They numb our feelings so it takes more and more excitement and drama (or even violence and cruelty) to feel alive. It is not much different than the patients I saw in the mental hospital who had to slit their arms with razors to feel alive.

On a chart, the daily ups and downs of these drama addicts might look like Figure 3. After a jolt cure, the change looks like Figure 4.

What the second curve reflects is just the normal ups and downs of living. But at first, recovering addicts and alcoholics interpret this as "God-awful boring and dull." They say things such as "If this is sobriety, who needs it."

It can take months or even years for an action addict to notice that there's actually a life going on along the curve they used to pass through on their rocket ride up to heaven or their inevitable descent into the pits. Slowly but surely, they adjust and learn to "smell the flowers" and notice what they've been missing all along. They begin to learn the art of living.

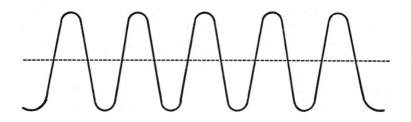

Figure 3

Figure 4

START LEARNING THE ART OF LIVING

Maintain (definition): To hold or keep in any state; to sustain; to preserve; to support; to defend.

—*Webster's*

Whenever I used to read about how this or that person had "really learned how to live" or had "mastered the art of living," I'd feel a stab of envy. I wasn't sure what "learning the art of living" meant, but it appealed to me. After I got sober, I began to understand that that's exactly what sobriety is all about. It's not about stopping drinking, or using, or smoking—that's just what we have to do as our ticket to get in. From then on, sobriety is a course in the art of life.

When we're out there "practicing our disease," as they say in the anonymous groups, and juggling crises, we don't have time for any of this. But in post-jolt sobriety we can finally begin to focus our attention on the larger issues of life, on grown-up things such as love and work, creativity, serenity, happiness, becoming better people, and having a little fun. We start to become what the psychologist Abraham Maslow called "self-actualized." Initially, we assume that everybody else has been self-actualized all along, and *we're* the ones who have to play catch-up. Later on we discover that most of the people who started off on this journey, like runners in a marathon, have peeled off somewhere. For whatever reasons, most people are unwilling or unable to hang in, so if you're still at it, give yourself a gold star.

COLLECT YOUR TIPS

> The process *starts* with the "beautiful moment." It's got to begin somewhere. Then it goes on from there.
> —*Gary Yontef, Ph.D., psychologist*

Wisdom, like sobriety itself, can come to us in big chunks, such as when we have a moment-of-clarity experience, or it can come to us in the form of "tips."

My own experience has been that after the initial jolt recovery that got me started, I've had to rely on tips to learn the rest, to learn the art of living. These tips have saved me. I pick them up everywhere, from other people, from recovery groups, from professional meetings, from books, from patients (out of the mouths of babes!), from articles, and from TV talk shows.

Here are some of my favorites:

Do What's Necessary

When it comes to maintaining your jolt healing, do whatever it takes. If it takes two AA meetings a day and 10 phone calls, that's what you do. Look at it this way: If you had a kidney disease and needed dialysis treatment three times a week for an hour—and if you didn't do it, you'd be dead in a week—wouldn't you do it? If the answer is yes, then look at your addiction the same way. So what if it's inconvenient to go to recovery-group meetings? What you *get* for your trouble is a decent life.

Don't Take the "First" Anything

Don't take the first drink, the first pill, the first fix, the first bite, the first bet, the first cigarette. Don't even make that first phone call to somebody with whom you're obsessed. It immediately gets your juices going, and suddenly you crave more. That's what addiction is. Don't poke a sleeping tiger with a stick.

H.A.L.T.

Another borrowed hint from the anonymous groups: Don't get too Hungry, too Angry, too Lonely, or too Tired. In other words, take care of yourself and eat your veggies. This makes sense for anybody, but for addicted people it can be a life saver, since excess stress can trigger slips, and slips can kill. Here's where I find "drama" helpful instead of hurtful. Looking at it in dramatic terms can force you to begin taking better care of yourself. Instead of the vague notion that you're doing it because it's "good for you," you're doing it to save your life.

The Only Two Reasons for Emotional Pain

When I was new in sobriety and still suffering emotional pain from my own "drama curve," a woman I went to for guidance told me: "There are only two reasons for emotional pain. One is because you're doing something you *shouldn't* be doing; the other is because you're *not* doing something you *should* be doing." It stopped me cold. That was sixteen years ago, and I've yet to come across a situation in which it doesn't apply. What it also does for me, even now, is help me focus on what actions I have to take to stop the pain. It's a truly handy concept. Try it.

Pain as Pusher

Pain is obviously what pushes us into action. But what if you decide not to take action? What if you do nothing? Or do *more* of what was causing you the pain? The answer is simple: You'll have more pain. Lots more pain. It will always be hovering over you, ready to take over. Eventually you'll have no choice. You'll have to kill the pain one way or another. Either you'll relapse— or you'll take action.

If you take action, you'll get to move on. If you relapse, then you'll get to go back to Go and start over again.

Now when some of my recovering patients come to me in great emotional pain, and I open my mouth to speak, they finish the sentence for me. They know what I'm going to say: "When it gets painful enough, you'll do something about it. . . ." That's always the way it is.

You're the Whole Pie, Not Just Pieces

For some reason I had the idea that being emotionally healthy and mature meant you got rid of all the bad things about yourself (like hostility, jealousy, pettiness) and you kept only the good things (responsibility, lovingness, generosity). Then at a workshop I heard a pop guru say of himself: "I am all things including bad." When he said that, I had a mini jolt experience. I went "Whew!" inside. It freed me. What he was saying was it's normal to have both bad and good things in our repertoire. What's important is how we behave. We don't have to get rid of our bad impulses; we just have to learn not to act on them. We have choices.

It was the beginning of my own self-acceptance. I hope it will help you with yours.

Memorize This: "No Matter What"

Inside the heart of every recovering addict, alcoholic, overeater, spender, gambler, or smoker, there lurks a Waiting One. This Waiting One is your addiction, and what your addiction is waiting for is an opportunity to win you back. Every time you're upset, every time you're in a brand-new situation, the Waiting One will be on hand in case *this* time you'll make an exception to the abstinence rule, in case *this* time you decide you've found a "reason" to drink again.

To fight the Waiting One, memorize this mantra and repeat it daily. Repeat it when you're upset. Repeat it when you have stress. Repeat it in every new situation: "We don't drink, we don't use—*no matter what.*" If you lose a job, you don't drink, you don't use—*no matter what.* If your relationship breaks up, you don't drink, you don't use—*no matter what.* If you're anxious, you don't drink, you don't use—*no matter what.* If somebody dies, you don't drink, you don't use—*no matter what.*

I think you get the idea. If you catch yourself looking for loopholes here, the way W. C. Fields did when somebody handed him a Bible, then you'd better take note of what you decide is your personal "exception" to the abstinence rule (defined in AA circles as freedom from alcohol *and* all other mind-altering chemicals). Think it through, because if you don't it could end up being your downfall.

If You Don't Want to Slip, Don't Go Where It's Slippery

This is another of AA's most basic survival rules. It's amazing how many people pay no attention to it: "Sure I went partying after I got out of treatment. I even went to a guy's house where there was this huge pile of cocaine on the coffee table—and I sat right near it. I even opened beers for other people just to prove to myself I was strong and could handle it without using."

Lots of luck, you idiot.

I hear this nonsense all the time, especially from men. My view is that life will throw us enough curves. We don't have to go looking for them. It's easy to be tough like this once, twice, maybe even 10 times. But the eleventh time will do you in. Sooner or later it'll suck you in just as if you'd been walking around and around the edge of quicksand.

So keep it simple: Don't go.

One Lifetime at a Time

This is just a personal quirk. What's a tip for one person falls on deaf ears for another. The "One Day at a Time" slogan never meant much to me. Besides, it's like holding out a carrot—"not today, but maybe *tomorrow*."

Rather than renegotiate this every morning, I prefer to do it once and for all and then forget about it. I stay away from alcohol and drugs, just like I stay away from jumping out of a nineteenth-floor window, "One Lifetime at a Time"—period. There's nothing more to discuss on this one.

Make Lists

One drawback of recovery is that we get responsible again. We start having jobs, friends, relationships, families, obligations, appointments—and we get totally overwhelmed.

The best treatment for being overwhelmed is the list. On a list, put all the things that are overwhelming you, all the things, both large and small, to which you have to attend. Then prioritize them, starting with number one for the most important and take it from there. Next take your number one item, write it on another piece of paper, and break it down into manageable segments. The term *manageable segments* is very important. It means you don't have to bite off more than you can chew. You can just take one little bite at a time.

Here's what one woman did. She went to the hardware store and bought a set of plastic drawers in which you can keep nails and things. (They come with eight drawers on up to 32, maybe more. If you have lots of problems, better pick one with lots of drawers.) Then she bought some three-by-five-inch file cards and counted out one for each drawer. On each card she wrote one of her problems and put it in its own drawer.

From then on, each morning she'd start the day by opening the drawers and taking out the cards. If there was something she could do that day about the problem on a card, she'd do it. If not, she'd put it back in the drawer and forget about it until the next day.

That's breaking something down into its manageable segments. Whether you do this literally or figuratively, by visualizing the drawers and file cards, it helps. I've been doing it by visualizing for years. Just picturing the drawers helps me remember that "overwhelmed" is made up of many parts (drawers), and each *part* is made up of parts—and I can start by handling just one of the parts.

Be Willing to Pay the Price

Somehow, somewhere, I got the notion that if you made the right decision there would be no price tag, and no pain. Therefore, if I had pain, it must be because I'd made the wrong decision. So I'd scramble to make another decision, with the same results. It drove me crazy.

I had it all wrong.

Once I got sober I learned the obvious—that everything, good and bad, costs something. Everything has a price tag. If you get married, you pay the price of losing your single state. If you go to the mountains, you miss a chance to swim in the sea. If you dull your feelings with drugs, you miss a chance to know how you react to things.

When I finally realized that everything, good and bad, has a price tag, it relieved and freed me. I no longer felt scared of my feelings. I realized I'm free to do anything I want—*if* I'm willing to pay the price. I think most addicts are capable of much more emotional pain than they think. It's thinking that it's "bad" to have emotional pain that makes us want to kill it off. Once we learn it's normal, we seem to be able to handle it.

Besides, some things are worth suffering a little pain for. That's called adventure!

Think the "Drink" Through to Its Logical Conclusion

Here's another tidbit of AA wisdom that can be applied to any number of situations. I've used it on my various addictions as well as on other things. It means to stop and consider the consequences of what you are about to do. I never used to want to do this. If it's a drink or a powdered-sugar donut, don't just think about how nice it would taste and how good it would feel, think about when it's finished. What then? How will you feel then? What are you likely to do next? Take another? And then what? What will your behavior be? How will others respond? How will you feel the next day? What effect will it have on your life and work?

Very often when people ask themselves these questions it stops them. They realize that they'd just been focusing on the pleasure part, not the consequences part.

Keep Perspective

It's easy to get self-centered and think we're the center of the universe, that our situation is really "serious." Some of us get into a "poor me" mode when something isn't working out the way we'd like. I find it handy to have little tricks to regain perspective, to see where my problem fits into the scheme of things. Reading the front page of the morning paper helps. In most cases I end up realizing I don't know what trouble is!

Another thing that helps me is a photograph on my wall of the planet Earth taken by the first astronauts on the moon. It makes the earth seem very small and unimportant. I look at the earth and try to imagine my "problem" as just a pinprick on the planet, and suddenly it doesn't loom quite so large.

"Grateful lists" help, too, corny as they sound. Write a list of 10 things you have/are for which you're grateful. Maybe you're better off than you thought compared with other souls on this earth.

Did you put "clean and sober" on your list?

Learn to Trust Your Gut

You've heard how important it is to "get in touch with your feelings" so often by now you probably want to gag. The trouble is, it's true. Wonderful as it is to have all the self-help groups, the anonymous programs, the sponsors and mentors, the addiction counselors, and the experts, there are times when it gets downright confusing. Nobody seems to agree with anybody else.

That's when you have to know what *you* think and what *you* feel, which isn't always an easy task if you've been stuffing your feelings and denying your intuition all these years.

Ultimately, you'll learn that the information you need to have a good life is already inside you. Some call this the God within. The trick is in seeing it, taking it seriously, and doing something about it.

Until you know yourself, you're going to be a sitting duck for others to dump on and try to influence. Do anything you can to speed up this inner journey. Therapy, groups, books, hypnosis. Anything—just do it.

Learn How to Just Say No

Once you learn how you feel about things, you begin to realize that you've been doing a lot of things you don't want to do and you've been spending time with people you don't want to spend time with. Now's the time to learn to say "no." But "no" turns out to be one of the most difficult words for the newcomer into sobriety or abstinence to say. The trouble is, *not* saying it can cause havoc. I want to recommend a book here that you can use as your "just say no" bible. It's called *When I Say No I Feel Guilty* by Manuel Smith, Ph.D. There are handy hints in there that could save your life.

I've developed some of my own guidelines: When people make a request of me and my stomach scrunches up, I read that as a definite "no" and try to act accordingly. If I can't "read" how I feel or know what I want clearly, I'll ask myself a question: "Am I looking forward" to whatever it is that they want me to do? I can usually answer that yes or no. Or I'll try to buy time: "Let me get back to you on that." I find that the minute I hang up or walk away and break the connection, I can think more clearly. When they're hovering over me or waiting for my answer, I may end up saying "yes" just to please them. That's called "people pleasing," and a lot of us do it. Buying time gives us a chance to realize that in many situations, we first have to please ourselves. Our sobriety may depend on it.

Push into the Red Zone

Nigerian folk wisdom says that a "bad dance doesn't kill the world." In other words, take a risk and push into new territory. Be a "Trekkie" and go where you've never gone before. Live a little. Try new things. Don't be afraid. Along the same lines AA says, "We don't get well gracefully," which means—so *what* if you make mistakes? It's only our ego that makes us think this is so terrible. Keep on keeping on. Sooner or later you'll get it right.

Do the Right Thing and Let the Chips Fall Where They May

Recovering addicted people are notorious for intellectualizing and over-analyzing: Should I do this or do that? Should I go here or go there? Should I say yes or say no? Yet most of us, beneath all this, really know right from wrong. I find it handy to ask myself, simply, "What's the *right* thing to do in this situation?" and then do it and let the chips fall where they may. Don't worry about how you "feel" about it. Do people worry about how Mother Teresa "feels" about her actions? No. The right actions speak for themselves. So if you really do the "right" thing, then the chips should fall in the right places and you should end up feeling just fine.

Later when you're helping others (we'll discuss this in the next chapter) you can appeal to their basic ethics and morals (which in the case of many alcoholics and addicts have been lying dormant for years) by asking them to make their new, sober decisions about things based on what the "right thing to do" is. Don't protect them, or yourself, from the truth here because, as English philosopher Herbert Spencer once said, "The ultimate result of shielding men from the effects of folly is to fill the world with fools." Now you wouldn't want to do that, would you?

Be Patient

You may have had your moment-of-clarity healing in an instant, but by now I'm sure you can see that maintaining the jolt cure and learning the art of living takes courage and time. If there's one magic word in all of this recovery business it's persistence. Persistence is the name of the game. Most people won't persist. They'll peel off and fall away. In the end, maybe 10 percent will make it and 90 percent won't. The choice is yours.

JUST ONE GLIMPSE OF HEAVEN

Years ago I read a newspaper article that touched me. It was about a man who had been deaf since childhood. He was working in a plant in which there was an explosion. He wasn't hurt at all. On the contrary, the explosion gave him his hearing back. He was in heaven. But then, only 24 hours later, he lost it again. The doctors had no explanation. The newspaper article ended with the comment that the man, now plunged back into his silence, was despondent. I never read anything more about it.

I've seen a similar thing happen to alcoholics and addicts who were jolted sober—and then lost it when they had a slip, and couldn't get it back again. It was as if they'd had a glimpse of heaven and then had it snatched away.

Hopefully it won't happen to you if you keep the story of that policeman in mind: *Don't forget.*

CHAPTER *14*

Helping Others

The Woman on the Bus

Some people come to Hollywood to be movie stars. I came to L.A. to rob and steal. I ended up on 5th Street sleeping behind trash cans. One day I was on a bus trying to sell stolen goods to a woman. She started talking to me: "I know all about who you are and what you're doing," she said, "and I think you should know that you don't have to go to the end of the line with it. You can stop this anytime at all." Then she wrote something on a piece of paper and handed it to me. It said: 1. Go to AA. 2. Ask for Fred. 3. Stay. 4. Ask them to send you to Acton Rehabilitation Center. I got off the bus, and for reasons I'll never understand, I followed her instructions. Today I don't sleep behind trash cans. Today I have my own business, and last summer, as president of the company, I went to Rome.

—Ralph, 60s, sober nine years

If 20 people cross your path in the course of a day, chances are that at least one of them is at some stage of a chemical-dependency problem. It could be a spouse, a parent, a child, a lover, a friend, an employee, a neighbor, or, as in the case of the woman on the bus, a stranger.

The addiction problem has become so big and so bad that we can no longer afford the luxury of not interfering or of minding our own business. The skid-row-bum's addiction problem is *our* addiction problem. On some level, perhaps, the woman on the bus knew this.

But what can you do? How can you make another person get jolted sober? Of course the answer to this is the same as the answer to the question of how you come up with a jolt cure for yourself: You can't make it happen, but you can help. You can take actions, sometimes a simple action such as speaking out, which may greatly increase the chance of triggering that all-important moment of clarity in another person.

In the case above, what if the man had missed the bus? Without getting into a variation of the darling-if-I-hadn't-gone-to-that-party-I-might-never-have-met-you game, there are two possibilities. One is that the man was so primed for recovery he'd have been triggered by something on the next bus. The other is that he was damn lucky. He was ready, *and* the woman intuitively said the right words that proved to be his last silver dollar and resulted in a jackpot, his sudden cure.

We can't do much about timing, but we can do something about recognizing when others are ready, and saying or doing whatever they might need us to say or do to trigger their healing response. What kind of helper or healer is most likely to be sensitive to these things? In the case of the woman on the bus, I suspect she was herself a recovering alcoholic. She was what we call a "wounded healer."

THE WOUNDED HEALER

> I was driving drunk and had an accident. The judge said, "I saw you in that play last night and you were so good I'd like to see you be in it again tonight, so I won't put you in jail." When I got home I got on my knees and said, "God, come into my life because I can't do it alone and for the rest of my life I'll *serve* you." That's what I've been doing and I've been alcohol free and drug free and pill free ever since.
> —*Diana Verona, actress, "Today Show," January 26, 1989*

There's a Greek myth about a man named Asclepius whose birth circumstances were unusual. His father was a god, and his mother was a mortal. One day while his mother was still pregnant with Asclepius, his father killed her in a jealous rage, cut her open, and ripped the baby from her womb. Asclepius, who was literally snatched from death, grew up to be a physician who saved others from death as he himself had been saved.

This tradition of becoming a healer (or in some cultures, a shaman or medicine man) after surviving an illness, a tragedy, or a near-death experience, is a common archetype and, as we've seen, is what Alcoholics Anonymous is based on. The magical healing forces appear to flow best through the person who has "been there."

Do you have to be a wounded healer to effectively help the addicted? This is a question that continues to be hotly debated. Nobody thinks a heart surgeon has to have had a heart attack in order to operate, but in addiction-recovery circles many believe that being a wounded healer is an important credential. Therapists and counselors who aren't themselves recovering don't like to hear this, of course, but I tend to agree that wounded healers have an edge. They have a "gut feel" for addiction and as a result seem more likely, either consciously or intuitively, to say or do something that can trigger a jolt cure in another.

Again and again I've seen nonrecovering helpers and healers (AA calls them "normies" or "civilians") blow it. Like well-schooled foreign agents, sooner or later they mispronounce a word, or they don't know something they *should* know, and they give themselves away. Suddenly they become "outsiders," which can make many addicted people just clam up. Wounded healers and wounded helpers rarely do the following: 1. speak of addicted people as "them," 2. put labels other than "alcoholic/addict" on anybody, 3. look for "reasons" the addiction happened in the first place, 4. let themselves be easily manipulated by the addicted person, 5. forget to keep the focus on the number one problem, which is the addiction, and let some other problem become number one, 6. buy into the addicted person's tendency to blame, project, deny, dramatize, and play victim, 7. fail to recognize that addicted people tend to "tune out" anybody who hasn't "been there," 8. either condone or prescribe mind-altering medications for addicted people who complain of anxiety, depression, or sleeplessness, 9. underestimate the power of obsession, and 10. underestimate the importance of a lifelong association with community self-help groups for lasting and comfortable addiction recovery.

Does that mean it's useless to try to help an addicted person if you yourself are not a wounded healer? Not at all; it just means that you have more to learn and that you have to work a little harder. The following tips may help.

TIPS FOR HEALERS, WOUNDED OR OTHERWISE

Whether you're a professional healer, such as a therapist or counselor, or an amateur healer, such as a spouse or a friend, what you do or say *can* affect and *can* potentially trigger a jolt cure in another human being. You should never say, "It won't do any good." If the woman on the bus had said, "It won't do any good," that man might still be robbing and stealing—and drinking.

Much of what I learned in graduate school about how to be a psychotherapist I've tossed out the window by now. I found that little of it applied to working with the addicted. What I've come up with instead is this list of tips, which can be used by professionals and nonprofessionals alike to help addicted others romance their jolt cures.

Tell Them About Moment-of-Clarity Recoveries

If you're trying to help an addicted person or people, whether you're a therapist or a friend, then by all means *tell* them that there is such a thing as a moment of clarity. Don't keep it a secret. Let them know that *they* can be jolted sober, no matter how many times they've tried in the past and failed. You have no idea how much hope this can offer. For some it will make the difference between giving up and hanging in. Now they know what they're hanging in *for*. Too often I hear things such as, "I went to AA. It didn't work." Answer this by telling them about the silver-dollar analogy and then ask: "If you put a silver dollar in a slot machine and didn't get a jackpot, would you say the slot machine didn't work?" That example usually makes its point right away.

It can also be helpful to get a person to think back and remember a time in the past when he or she might have had an experience similar to a moment of clarity—an aha! of some kind, such as a sudden solution to a school or work problem. Once people can identify even a little bit with what the moment-of-clarity event feels like, they're usually willing to concede that it exists and might even happen again in the area of their addiction.

Here's the case of a woman who was getting discouraged in the pre-jolt phase but became willing to hang in once it was pointed out that since she'd had a jolt cure in another area before, it could probably happen to her again.

Patient: I had an instant healing with my smoking, but I can't seem to do it with my weight.
Therapist: How did you do it with smoking?
Patient: I went to a group.
Therapist: Have you been to a group for weight?
Patient: Well, I did go to OA a couple of times, but I couldn't stick with it. It was hard.
Therapist: It was hard because you hadn't had your moment of clarity. Go back there. Put your body where they're talking about your primary problem and keep it there, even when it's hard, even if you're gaining weight instead of losing. Sooner or later you'll hear something that will trigger your jolt healing. After that you won't find it hard. It'll get easier.
Patient: (Suddenly identifying with what therapist is saying) Yes! Now I understand, because that's just what happened with the smoking. I tried and failed many times, but once I had that shift inside, it was no longer hard. Okay, I'll go back to OA!

Tell Them About the Seven Ways to Romance Jolt Cures

Once you've got their attention by telling them about the moment of clarity, the next thing to do is tell these people about the seven ways of romancing it. Usually they'll ask: "How can I make a jolt cure happen?" Don't make promises. Tell them the truth—that nobody can make it happen, but that they can significantly increase their chances by their actions. Go over the seven romance methods with them. Discuss each one, get their feedback and with that, combined with your own "gut feel," determine which ways might give them the best shot at healing. Are they people oriented? Book oriented? Body oriented? Do what this addiction therapist does:

> I spray my patients with questions and all kinds of suggestions, and I don't give up. There are some patients who have to be hit with just the right words and just the right game plan before something happens.
>
> *—Jim, counselor, sober 22 years*

Here's another therapist with a similar approach:

> I try to expose my patients to things like AA to increase the possibility of their having a moment of clarity. I encourage patients to fill their cups to overflowing. Some come in with fuller cups than others, so for them it takes less time.
>
> *—Barbara Kearney, psychotherapist*

This next therapist seems to have a pretty levelheaded view of the role he plays in the jolted-sober experience:

> I can't make somebody have the experience; that's an act of grace, but I can set up the environment to make it feasible. I think the moment of change comes from the unconscious. I view my work as a therapist as creating the situation to ripen my patients for the sudden healing experience. I try to become sensitive to where the experience might lurk.
>
> *—Eric Marcus, M.D., psychiatrist*

Observe the Addicted on Their Own Turf

Even if the particular person you're concerned about won't go to treatment, *you* go. Go to your own treatment, which might be Al-Anon, the self-help group for family and friends of alcoholics, and go to *his or her* treatment also. By this I mean specifically, go to AA, CA, NA, OA, GA, or whatever other "A" is appropriate. Most larger communities have meetings that are open to friends, relatives, students, and professionals.

If you're not a wounded healer yourself, if you haven't "been there," this is by far the best way to get a feel for addiction. It's better than books, better than graduate school, better than anything else I can think of. Every doctor and every therapist should have to attend at least 100 AA meetings before they even talk to an addicted person.

The more you know addiction with your heart, not your head, the better able you'll be to say or do what you need to say or do to help somebody else be jolted sober.

Never Talk to Somebody Right After a "Fix"

One of the worst times to communicate with addicted persons is right after they've had a "fix" of whatever their drug of choice is. I've even discovered that it's useless to talk to patients in obsessive relationships right after they've been with the person with whom they're obsessed. A woman obsessed with a married man can't be reasoned with when she's still in the afterglow of his phone call. Even that is a "fix." And it takes time for the fix to wear off, for the pain of withdrawal to set in again. No pain, no ears. They just won't listen.

The best time to get to them is when they're hurting. "Kick 'em when they're down!" is how one addiction therapist puts it. Blunt but true. Kick 'em when they're hung over. Kick 'em when they feel guilty. Kick 'em when they're scared.

All healers and helpers should know about and take advantage of the Hitting Bottom phenomenon we talked about in Chapter 12.

Here's a man who "hit bottom" back in the 1700s because of embarrassment. It was reported by Benjamin Rush, one of the first people to call alcoholism a "disease" and the physician who was trying to help this "hopeless" alcoholic:

> One morning, hungover, he witnessed one of his servants entertaining the others by mimicking him when he was drunk. The sight overwhelmed him with shame and distress, and reformed him.

Without intending to, the servant had kicked him when he was down.

Don't Expect Credit

I once heard a teacher say that when the children she taught understood what she was saying, she could see blue light coming out of their heads.

Now that's what I call getting feedback. Unfortunately, most of us aren't likely to get feedback from our helping efforts with the addicted, so don't expect it. Don't be like the psychiatrist who published an article in a psychiatric journal complaining about ungrateful patients who don't give their doctors the credit for their improvements. He cited the case of a woman patient who came into a session and told him that what had helped her with a specific problem was a remark her sister made. The psychiatrist was bent out of shape about this. He felt it was hostile of his patient not to credit him. Obviously what happened is she'd had a moment of clarity, triggered by her sister's remark, and she'd given the credit to her sister. It's a natural mistake. Had she and the psychiatrist been aware of the moment-of-clarity phenomenon, they'd have understood this. He might even have been able to be "big" enough to smile about it and *let* her give credit to her sister. At least he'd know his input and the work they'd done in their sessions had played a part. The sister was just this patient's last silver dollar, that's all.

But it all evens out in the end. Sometimes therapists get credit where it's not due. This has happened to me more than once. Patients have a moment of clarity in my office or soon afterward, and *I* get the thanks for being "brilliant." I know better, but that's how it feels to them and they won't hear otherwise. They often want to believe you "did" it.

Here's a situation in which a child's remark in a therapist's office did the trick. Here, too, the therapist (who knew better) got the credit:

> I was doing an intervention with the family of an alcoholic father. He was there in the session, a big, burly, scary kind of guy. At one point during the interview, which was going nowhere, the man's six-year-old son jumped up into his lap and said, "Daddy, maybe you wouldn't smell so bad if you quit drinking." The man has been sober ever since. The family kept telling me I was the marvelous one, but that remark from that child is what did it.
>
> —*story told by a Manhattan addiction counselor*

Here's a similar case, this one involving a hospital chaplain who got the credit for saving the day by calming an upset relative:

> Doctors won't admit it, but in this healing business it's all timing. I don't think we choose the time: we're chosen. I realized this when a crazy man whose wife had just died came in to talk to me. He was angry. I was afraid of him. I thought he was going to clobber me. Then he went into the chapel—I don't know what happened to him in there, but when he came out he was entirely different. The doctors couldn't thank me enough, but I didn't do a thing.
>
> —*hospital chaplain, Los Angeles*

Don't Bite Your Tongue

> I fought myself and tried to bite my tongue. I kept thinking, "Diane, you just can't say something like that to a dying old lady!" But the impulse just wouldn't go away. Finally I just burst out,

"Mother, if you *want* to drink yourself to death, go right ahead. We'll be fine." I wasn't being sarcastic. I really meant it. Suddenly she looked so relieved, as though now I'd given her permission to decide if she wanted to live or not for *herself*, not because we needed her. "I think I'll live," she said matter of factly.

—Diane, 40s, herself sober 15 years

The more in touch you are with your own feelings, the better able you'll be to trust your gut when dealing with an ill person—just as Diane was in the conversation with her mother. You don't have to struggle so hard to bite your tongue because sometimes what you blurt out is just what the addicted person needs to hear to have a moment-of-clarity healing. So trust what your insides tell you to say. The message needs you to be the messenger. More than one healing has been triggered by somebody else's throwaway line.

It could also be something you're trying *not* to feel that does it. In the next quote, a woman was trying not to let her aunt know how upset she was about the aunt's self-destructive drinking:

I was trying to be rational and loving and supportive and wise on the phone, and all of a sudden I just burst into tears. It was a surprise to both of us. Up until that moment, my aunt had been fighting me. Suddenly she stopped and calmly agreed to keep the appointment with the addiction counselor that I'd set up for her.

—Edie, 46

Have a "Sobriety Brochure" On You

We keep telling people they have to get clean and sober without telling them what sobriety is like. That's like landing in a foreign country without having seen the brochure.

When I got sober I had no idea what sobriety was like. I stopped drinking to stop the pain, not to *get* sober. I thought sobriety meant life without liquor. Period. I didn't know about the good things.

What I've learned from this is that it's important for some people to have a picture of the land of sobriety painted for them before they make the trip. This is one thing AA and the other anonymous groups are able to do—paint this picture. Sometimes it's the hope offered by the news that sobriety is actually fun that gives people the courage to try it. That in itself can trigger a moment of clarity, during which the willingness to take that risk is found.

Leave Them Alone

"Do something for someone you love today; leave them alone."

Al-Anons tell this to one another as a reminder that there are times to stop trying to fix other people and let them be.

Sometimes the best way to get others to have a moment of clarity is to do nothing. Stop pushing. Let them be. Let them be still long enough to begin to hear their inner voices, to possibly get their moment of clarity as a result of something that happens within. Don't distract people with your words when it's their own words to which they need to attend. Here's a woman who figured this out:

> My moment of clarity came after another of my husband's drunken rages. I realized in a flash that I'd emerge from the tunnel in which we now lived only if I focused on *my* problems, not his. Within the hour I made a phone call to Al-Anon and with that call my own recovery began. It resulted in a change in the climate of our household. A few years later my husband found sobriety.
> —*Olga, 50s*

Respect Resistance

If the person you're helping, whether he's sober or not, resists one of your suggestions, it could mean one of two things. Either he doesn't know what's good for him—or he does.

I was trained in the tradition that patients don't know anything. They don't know how they feel or what's right for them. In other words, therapists are always right and patients are always wrong. I no longer believe this. I now believe that inside every addicted person, even the sickest of them, even the far-gone crack case, there's that little inner physician who knows best how *that* particular addict can be healed. So I always listen to what an alcoholic or addict says about his case. I hear out his rationalizations, his protests, his excuses, the reasons why he can't do A and needs to do B—just in case something suddenly "feels right." After all, if the purpose of therapy is to know oneself, then it's got to start somewhere.

Perhaps 95 percent of the time I conclude that patients really don't know themselves, but occasionally I'm surprised. They'll do it their way, and a jolt cure is the result—like the businessman who checked out of the hospital before he'd finished treatment to go to a convention. We were all convinced he'd drink again because he was anything but committed to sobriety. But while there, something triggered his moment of clarity and he returned, sober, to finish treatment, and has been sober ever since. Things like this can be humbling—or exciting, depending on how you look at them. I think it's fun to find them exciting.

Be Patient, Teach Patience

Even though we're talking here about "instant cures," we have to make it clear to those we help that the preparation for that magic moment takes time, so they should plan to wait it out and not quit five minutes before the miracle. Maybe a good rule of thumb is two years. Once people show an interest in changing, it will probably be a good two years until they're ready for a jolt cure. Here's a "wounded healer" counselor who agrees, based on her own experiences:

> The moment of clarity is a natural process, a matter of individual timing, and it has to be respected. I can predict within about two years when someone's first one will happen. Usually right *before* it they get into a very negative state, that's how I know. That's the

time to encourage them to hang in because that's just when some people want to run.

—*Deborah S., sober 11 years*

Go One More Round

Some of the addicted people you work with will have a jolt healing, which is exciting. It's a reward for you as well as for them. Some of the addicted people you work with will get clean and sober for a while, but not because of a jolt cure. They'll bite the bullet and be uncomfortable. That's frustrating. At least their heads will be clear so they can work with you on romancing the jolt cure that they still need to get over the hump.

Some people, unfortunately, just aren't going to make it at all. I've stopped predicting which ones they'll be. There's really no way to tell. Whenever I try to drag out my crystal ball, I end up wrong as often as I do right, so I've given up on the predicting game. I sleep better that way.

Not everybody is destined to be jolted sober, which isn't always an easy thing to accept. Alcoholics Anonymous is philosophical about it: "Some must die so that others may live."

The thing is, when it comes to working with others, just as when you're working on your own addiction, if you don't try, if you don't go in there for one more round, you won't know whether or not the next moment was *the* moment.

To me, the moment-of-clarity approach to addiction healing gives hope. No matter how many times you've tried, no matter how many times you've failed, there's always hope. There is always a chance that something can come out of left field and trigger a lifelong moment of clarity in even the most unlikely candidates.

If you're skeptical, ask the man who got on that bus.

CHAPTER *15*

FutureJolt

> Stay sober, and you can have a healthy life, a joyous
> heart—and a piece of the action.
>
> —*Hal, 30s, sober 11 years*

It has been more than sixteen years since I was jolted sober.
Research-wise, three main things have happened since I first
started tracking this moment-of-clarity thing. One, I've gotten
better at unearthing existing information about sudden healing. I "discovered," for example, Eastern writings, the mystics,
William James, Richard Bucke, and the contributions of Christian Science and other philosophies. Two, I've become more
skilled at listening with that "third ear" therapists talk about.
Today when people tell about addiction healing experiences I
can hear what they're really saying, no matter what words they
use, whereas before I was oblivious to them. Three, I've been
helped by the fact that over the past decade much more information about moment-of-clarity experiences has become available. The West has fallen in love with the East, and as a result
we've been inundated with Eastern thinking and literature. And
of course since the East has always been open to the idea of
instant change, it's made us more open to it. In addition, the
holistic health movement started, as did the New Age movement, and both of them brought new publications and helped
us see quick healing in a less blasphemous light.

IS HUMAN NATURE CHANGING?

Buddhism says there have already been thousands of Buddhas (enlightened beings who have had moment-of-clarity experiences in the spiritual sphere) walking the earth. And certainly there are hundreds of thousands of people alive right now who have had jolt cures from addictions. Does that mean that jolt cures are becoming more common? Is human nature changing? Will our children and grandchildren be biologically more susceptible to sudden healing? After all, over the millennia we've learned to smell better and to differentiate more colors, so why shouldn't we learn to heal better?

Richard M. Bucke, M.D., who wrote the book *Cosmic Consciousness*, claims that so-called spiritual experiences *are* increasing and will continue to do so. Certainly, acceptance of them is increasing. Bucke also believes that the moment-of-clarity event may even turn out to be the salvation of humankind. And sociologists tell us that when 20 percent of the population finally accepts a new idea (and you could say that instant recovery from addiction is still a "new" idea) it becomes unstoppable. In other words, there may come a day when the existence of a quick fix for addiction will be assumed. We will no longer be told: There's no such thing as an instant cure.

"I don't know if instant cures have increased," said one therapist friend of mine, "but I sure know that *talking* about them has increased. Almost everybody I meet has had one—or several."

THE FUTURE OF JOLT CURES

In my crystal ball (no doubt made from melted-down gin bottles) I can see a day when having and teaching about jolt healings will be commonplace. We'll have Jolt Cure workshops and treatment programs. We'll have How to Be Jolted Sober classes in high schools, jolt-healing directories, and adult education classes at the "Y" to instruct people on how to help a loved one have a jolt-recovery experience.

Even if *none* of that happens, the jolted-sober concept turns out to be quite practical, and it has given us many gifts.

GIFTS OF THE JOLTED-SOBER EXPERIENCE

It Clears Up Confusion

One day at the chemical-dependency treatment center where I work as a therapist, I decided that instead of "group" we'd watch a TV talk show billed as "The Controversy Over Alcoholism."

We all gathered around the set and watched as six guests debated with the audience and each other about such questions as: Is alcoholism a disease? Is it inherited? Or is it a purely psychological problem? Does AA "work"? Does hospitalization "work"? If treatment is so important, then how come some people get better all on their own?

One guest told how he cured himself without treatment.

> I quit [drinking] over two years ago while I was sitting in a courtroom [for a drunken driving arrest]. My lawyer came up to me and said, "I can get you a conditional discharge." I said, "What are the conditions?" He said, "That you don't drink again for a year—then you *might* get your license back." And I swear, that moment, sitting in that courtroom on that wooden bench, I swore I'd never touch another drop. And I have not even had the *urge* to have another drink since then.
>
> —*Dan, sober two years*

This story created more debate: If somebody can cure himself, does it mean he wasn't really an alcoholic in the first place? Does it mean that AA is useless and that expensive treatment is a hoax? Are we telling people they're alcoholic when they're not? Is this a conspiracy?

Round and round they went and it was frustrating to sit listening to it knowing what we know. (We'd had a group discussion about moment-of-clarity jolt cures only days before.) It was clear to us that the man who said he'd cured himself in the courtroom had really had a jolt cure that he was taking full credit for, a cure that could have happened anywhere—even at an AA meeting. Interestingly enough, he did say that he goes to AA now. Instinctively, he realized that jolt cures have to be maintained.

The next time the man mentioned he'd gotten sober on his own, one of our patients shouted back at the TV: "You had a moment of clarity, bozo!" To us it seemed obvious.

Viewing the jolted-sober experience as the common denominator here, some of what they were arguing about can be cleared up. Whenever somebody is jolted sober, whatever treatment setting they're in (or not in) "works." Nothing works for the person who doesn't have a jolt cure. It works no matter what the "cause" is determined to be, whether it's genetic, psychological, environmental. The cure transcends the causes—making them interesting, perhaps, but irrelevant. And of course the "best treatment" (they all debated over this one) is clear: It's whatever triggers the moment of clarity.

This is why I find the jolted-sober concept so useful. It explains some things we've been baffled about for a long time.

It Legitimizes Quick Cures

I was trained that there is no such thing as a quick cure from addiction. Then I had one (alcoholism), followed two years later by a second (smoking). Then I began to observe them all around me, and my historical research proved to me that they've always been here. That we failed to notice them was our limitation. We're not so blind anymore. The overwhelming evidence for the existence of jolt cures for addiction has finally sunk in. They are becoming legitimized instead of discounted. If the only thing you pick up from this book is the fact that jolt cures *do* exist, that alone can help you. It gives you something to hang on to. There's light at the end of the tunnel after all.

It Encourages Taking Action

> When you have to make a choice and don't make it, that in itself is a choice.
>
> —*William James, psychologist*

Even though we can't make a moment of clarity happen, the jolted-sober concept lets us know that when it comes to curing our addiction we're anything but helpless. In fact, it's our responsibility to get up and take actions to bring a recovery on, instead of sitting around waiting for "happenstance" to strike us healed. No more whining: "It's useless," and "nothing works" when in truth *every*thing works if the timing is right. The French film director Jean Cocteau once compared drug-taking to getting out of a train while it is still moving. "It is to concern oneself with something other than life, with death," he said.

So let's get up and start concerning ourselves with life.

It Eliminates the Search for the "Best Treatment"

Since we've learned that it's the triggers, not the treatments, we're after, we don't have to waste our time looking for the best treatment in town with the highest success rate. We just have to worry about making ourselves a "fertile field" (by going to lots and lots of recovery group meetings, for example) so we'll be primed. Then, when the right stimulus comes along, it will have a better chance of being that last silver dollar we need for the jackpot.

So even if you're out in Nowhere Flats, you can still be jolted sober, no matter what your addiction, simply by doing whatever romance method is available to you and giving it a fair try.

It Gives Us Words to Communicate About It

Terms like jolt cure and moment of clarity may not be ideal, but they are among the best we've got to date to describe this fascinating phenomenon of instant addiction healing. They are to addiction what the term spontaneous remission is to physical disease. At least the terms make it clear that the phenomenon exists, that it's legitimate and can be worked for.

It Shows Us Our Personal History Is Not Our Destiny

The jolted-sober concept is encouraging because it shows us that our past history doesn't determine whether or not we'll get sober and stay that way. No matter how many times we've tried and failed in the past, we can still have a lasting jolt cure. Our history is irrelevant. The moment of clarity severs our tie with our past in one discontinuous leap.

It Eliminates the "New Sin" of Self-Blame

One negative bit of fallout from the New Age movement is the idea that since our brains supposedly affect our bodies, then therefore if we get a physical illness such as cancer we're at fault because we had the "wrong thoughts" or "wrong emotions." It's a blame-the-victim thing, which is nonsense. It rests on the mistaken assumption that it's our conscious thinking that affects our bodies, whereas it's more likely our *un*conscious thinking that does so. Over this we have no control. The jolted-sober concept, on the other hand, never once says it's the conscious mind that creates a moment of clarity, therefore there's no "blame" if we can't *make* it happen. All we can do is romance it. Remember why we picked the word *romance* in the first place? Because there are no guarantees.

It Relieves Us of the "Fighting Spirit" Requirement

For those who've assumed they could never have a jolt cure because they don't "really believe" in it or don't have "faith," the moment-of-clarity concept probably comes as a relief because it doesn't require belief and faith. This also eliminates the sticky question of how one manages to acquire this faith if one doesn't start out with it. This means that skeptics, atheists, and nay-sayers are no longer disenfranchised. They, too, can be jolted sober. The fighting spirit turns out to be an outcome rather than a prerequisite of the moment-of-clarity experience, but because it all happens instantaneously, most people put the cart before the horse. In my case, my faith level before my recovery was zilch. What gave me "faith" was being jolted sober.

It Lets Us Drop Our "Why" Search

Here I am, sober for over sixteen years and a psychotherapist to boot, which means that looking for "whys" is my business. Yet when it comes to my own addiction I *still* don't know why I drank. I used to think this why business was important, that without it I couldn't achieve sobriety. (I once read an article in a psychiatric journal in which the author, a psychoanalyst, claimed that alcoholism in women stems from a fear of birds!) Then I had my jolt cure and realized that my "reasons" why and my history, as I said above, were irrelevant. One thing the moment of clarity can do (or so it seems at the time) is return you back to your original choice-point (to drink, or not to drink) and let you re-choose this time *not* to be addicted. In a way, it's like the past gets rewritten so you really have no need to investigate your "other" past. This new one works better.

What a relief this can be for people who think they've got years and years of probing into the psyche ahead of them. They can instead concentrate on one of the Seven Ways to Romance a Jolt Recovery.

Later, after the jolt cure, if anyone wants to backtrack and muck around their background or their brain for entertainment, or see a therapist for other problems, fine, but when it comes to addiction recovery it's not necessary.

It Offers Hope

Currently, addiction treatment is marked by lots of discouragement. The true recovery rates are dismal, and in their heart of hearts most people know this, no matter what the treatment center commercials and treatment program brochures say. So the addicted people get discouraged, and the people who love them get discouraged. Especially if they've tried getting sober once or twice and "failed."

But the moment-of-clarity concept lets the alcoholic, the addict, the gambler, the overeater, know that an "instant" healing can still happen at any time. So they need to hang in and be patient. They may have to spend years in the pre-jolt phase just preparing for their jolt cure. Why this is, nobody knows. Nobody knows why some people get well quickly and some take a long time at it. Nobody knows just how many times a specific person will have to go to an AA meeting, or meditate, or jog, or talk to somebody, before their own self-healing powers finally get triggered by something and suddenly go to work. Nobody knows why one person can walk by a slot machine, casually drop in a silver dollar and hit a jackpot, while another can put in his or her life savings and end up with nothing. Maybe there's a formula to that one, but we haven't caught onto it yet. What we do know is that we can no more say that a particular treatment we've picked "doesn't work" than we can say that the slot machine we've dropped a coin into "doesn't work" if we don't hit the jackpot. So we just have to keep dropping in those coins until something happens.

But thanks to our new knowledge of the jolt cure, at least we know that if we do hang in, total healing is very possible.

Recently I heard a woman speak out at a self-help discussion group for alcoholics. She sounded like somebody who understood what the jolted-sober concept was all about and it was keeping her from running away. It offered her hope:

> I'm not discouraged. I've had one slip after another, but at least I'm better off than I was a year ago when I was drinking every day. I *know* I'm going to get sober eventually. I know something is going to *click* sooner or later. I consider this year a learning experience that I can turn around and share with others someday. I just have to do the footwork, and I know I'll end up being okay.
>
> —*woman, 30s, at a recovery group meeting*

It Reminds Us That Mysteries Still Exist

> There are more things in heaven and earth, Horatio, than are dreamt of in your philosophy.
>
> —*Shakespeare*, Hamlet, *Act I, Scene 5*

No matter how hard we've looked for something to explain the phenomenon of instant healing, the answer keeps eluding us. The Alister Hardy Research Center, even after studying and categorizing all those thousands of cases, admits that they, too, still haven't been able to get to the essence of the so-called spiritual experience, which remains elusive and ineffable. Nor have any of the other great thinkers of our time—the psychologists, philosophers, religionists, and physicists—managed to come up with any explanations. They all keep coming back to the same conclusion: Instant healing is a mystery. And it looks like it's a mystery that's going to be with us for a while. The cosmic joke here, of course, is that even though we don't understand instant healing it "works" anyway.

Besides, we need mysteries. What fun would it be if we didn't have any? The fact that the world is still full of unanswered questions is one of the things that makes life exciting. If we knew it all, then what would we do? Jung himself said that our world view should always include in it a place for the improbable. And the whole idea that a complex illness, such as addiction, can disappear in a split second is most certainly "improbable."

However, when you have your own moment of clarity you'll no longer think of a quick cure as improbable. You'll think of it as true.

> I'd failed so often people were shunning me. I remember lying there in detox, one more time, when suddenly it was as though I saw myself sitting across the room in a chair, and I was able to forgive myself for all my relapses. Everything got light in the room. It was as though I had this rock I was carrying around and all of a sudden I just let it go and I knew everything was going to be all right. I felt ten feet tall, like no matter what happened in my life from this moment on, I'd be able to handle it. And I said to myself, "It's all an adventure now."
>
> *—Reggs, 40s, sober one year*

So let's get on with the adventure.

Index

acupressure, 77
acupuncture, 8, 77
addiction
  professionals' ignorance of, xii
  seen as symptom, xii
aha! experience, 1, 92, 117
Al-Anon, 119, 123
Alcoholics Anonymous, xvi, 1, 3, 4, 7, 9,
    29, 43, 47, 52, 53, 84, 86, 98, 99, 103,
    105, 108, 110, 113, 115, 119, 123, 128,
    133
  agnostics in, 32
  Big Book of, 15, 20, 35, 61
  membership statistics, xvi, 3
  paradoxes in, 8, 84–85
  recovery statistics, 125
  "wounded healers" in, 115
animal magnetism, 28
Asclepius, 114–115
aversion therapy, 84, 89

biofeedback, 8, 65, 78–79
"biting the bullet," xv, 125
born-again experience, 5, 67. See also
    moment-of-clarity
Boston State Hospital, xi
brain
  and the moment-of-clarity, 35–38
  biochemistry of, 74–75
  nondrug ways to alter, 76
  shift, 5, 11
  ways to romance moment-of-clarity,
    8, 73–80
Breisser, Arnold, Ph.D., 85
Bridges, William, 86
Bucke, Richard M., M.D., 11, 126, 127
Buddha, transformation of, 14
Buddhism, 127
bulimia, 61, 68
"burden lifted" phenomenon, 19–20

cancer, 37, 131
Castaneda, Carlos
  on hesitation, 10
"causeless" events, 11–14, 75
cause(s)
  cultural need for, 13–14
chemistry, brain, 8. *See also* brain
  chemistry
Christ, Jesus, 25, 31
Christian Science, 27, 126
"civilian(s)," 115
click, xiii, 1, 11
  see also moment-of-clarity
Cocaine Anonymous (CA), 46, 119
Cocteau, Jean, 130
collective unconscious, 28
computer/brain analogy, 73–74
Conrad, Barnaby, 3
consequences, 88. *See also* punishment
contrary ways to trigger moment-of-
    clarity, 8, 81–85
conversion experience, xi, 14, 29. *See*
    also moment-of-clarity
convictional experience, 5. *See also*
    moment-of-clarity
Cousins, Norman, 37, 74

Dark Ages, 24–26
denial, 62–63, 90
Descartes, Rene, 36
discontinuous events, 13, 131
divine intervention, 5, 30, 31
dual addictions, 54
dualism, 36–37
"drama curve," 100–101
dreams, 8

Eastern thinking, influence of, 126
Einstein, Albert, 50
endorphins, 35, 36, 51, 78